I0491638

BUILDING REAL WORLD PHP APPLICATIONS

PHP HTML MYSQL PRACTICAL COURSE FOR BEGINNERS

©2021 Andrea Mauro Raimondi

AREdit.com

For contacts and requests info@aredit.com

<?php Building Real World PHP Applications ?>

BUILDING REAL WORLD PHP APPLICATIONS

PHP HTML MYSQL PRACTICAL COURSE FOR BEGINNERS

©2021 Andrea Mauro Raimondi

AREdit.com

For contacts and requests info@aredit.com

{2}

<!=== Andrea Mauro Raimondi ===>

To Filippo and Massimiliano

Programming is a technique.
Know how to write applications,
think about them,
find solutions
it is an art.

<?php Building Real World PHP Applications ?>

<!=== Andrea Mauro Raimondi ===>

INDEX

<?php Building Real World PHP Applications ?>

<!=== Andrea Mauro Raimondi ===>

INTRODUCTION

Learning to program can take place in many ways that we can insert into two main strands: academically, learning the grammar and syntax of a language, or learning by doing, working directly on a concrete project.

Certainly, in a given moment the two paths meet: it is natural to deepen more and more the language that is used as we work with it.

Working directly on a complete project, I will try to focus on the fundamental aspects of PHP language. The goal is to allow the reader to become autonomous, and works on projects, more and more complex. It is the challenges won, the effort to find solutions to a problem, which advances knowledge and which pushes the programmer to want to deepen the programming theory.

We will immediately work on the building of an online catalog. This will allow us to address both the problems relating to the design and construction of a reserved area, the back office, and the building of a public website.

My encounter with web programming dates back to the late 1990s. At the time, most of the websites, "showcase" sites, were built almost exclusively with HTML. Pages and pages of .html files and HTML pages of product sheets. Every modification, even of a comma to be inserted in pages' header, had to be repeated for all the product sheets. Dozens of times. This was my first job: write Html pages. There were already visual editors like FrontPage or Dreamweaver (who remembers them?), But I worked for a

<?php Building Real World PHP Applications ?>

strange gentleman, the bearer of a Zen philosophy in web programming: go to the gist of things, to the essential core. You worked directly on text files, with text editors. Arachnophilia was used in that company, it still exists and I recommend it too. At the time we worked with Window95. After a while, I fell in love with open source, Linux, and *BSD, operating systems. Today's versions of Linux have grown enormously and spread and are not comparable to the programming school they were twenty years ago. From the open-source world, Apache, the webserver, has become the most widespread in the server world, and the PHP language, born from the web, for the web, is now used everywhere. For us, in that small company in Milan, always looking to reduce costs, it was a boon. After the first "dynamic" applications, as it was said at the time, using Microsoft's ASP web language, and MS Access as a database. ASP was the language through which I learned the basics of building web applications. We then embraced PHP and the database server MySQL. At the time, the web was a land of bloody battles between browsers, between MSInternetExplorer and Netscape Navigator, between jpg and gif images, with the smallest possible dimensions: we traveled at 56k if all went well. There were modems and their typical connected data exchange sound. And we were already a thousand times ahead of textual BBS.

Throughout my career, I have faced and built many projects, from the simplest, such as showcase sites, to complex ones, such as entire management systems starting from scratch. Much was customized on the client's requests. Today, where everything seems al-

<!=== Andrea Mauro Raimondi ===>

ready exist, that everything is already built, where there are web apps that contain everything, but which are used only for a fraction of their potential, it seems that we are looking for more simplicity, we are going back to looking for what we need in a business. For this reason, I think it is useful to understand the basis mechanisms of a web application and create software that serves, that solves the real needs and problems of a customer or a business.

Programming means creating. It is the work of ancient craftsmen, and creating web applications gives you the same satisfaction as creating an object that will later be useful to someone. We will learn by doing and deepen by doing.

<?php Building Real World PHP Applications ?>

<!=== Andrea Mauro Raimondi ===>

PART I
Starting project

WHAT WE NEED TO START

A PHP-based web application needs two elements to exist: a web server that processes PHP pages and a database that maintains data over time. By its nature, a web page does not maintain status. It does not store data. With the development of browsers and memory capabilities, this has been partially overcome.

So we need a web server capable of handling PHP.

You can download and install a webserver program like Apache on your computer. On the internet, you will find the latest versions and installation details. And for our purposes, we will use the MySQL database server to store the data. You can download and install it in both Windows and Linux versions.

We will use a text program to write the code. I use Kate. Any other editor is good.

Always remember that the final result of our PHP pages is given by an HTML page. The web server returns an HTML page. See Appendix for more details on how to install Apache, PHP, and MySQL.

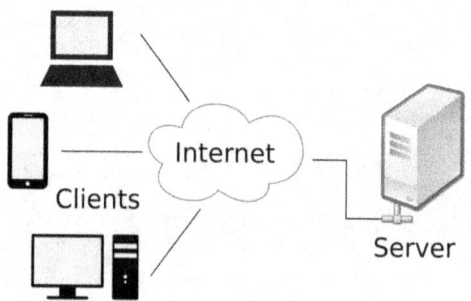

<!=== Andrea Mauro Raimondi ===>

HOW TO BUILD A WEB APP
THE THEORY

A web app or web-based application is software that essentially lives through a web server and a client/server interaction that we have seen before.

It must have a purpose. It must do something. It can be a simple showcase site for viewing a product catalog, a website to manage the content of text and images. It can be a management software that, for example, keeps track of goods in stock, produces documents, performs analysis and reports. In all cases, we have different levels of interaction with the application, based on how the data is processed: who can see them, who can process them, insert them, modify them, delete them. Besides, some areas of the software may only be accessible at certain authorization levels.

It is, therefore, necessary to understand what is the purpose of the project and what are data to be treated. What is their flow, how they must move, what they must do; who will have to manage this data, i.e. how many authorization levels we can have; how the data will be handled, i.e. who can do what with the data. The analysis phase is the most important phase of the whole project.

Then we have to create the database, create the folders on the server, create the PHP / HTML code based on the database and the data movement.

In our project, our customer is a thrift store that wants to put its catalog online. After the interview with the customer, we understood that the data to be managed are fundamental of two types:

<?php Building Real World PHP Applications ?>

the categories of articles and the various articles. We then go into the details of each type of data. For the categories, it is sufficient to indicate the name of the category itself: turntable, records, cassettes, CDs, etc. For the objects, we will indicate, the title, the image, the description, and the cost. To make those who insert the data autonomously, we will build a back-office area in which the data will be entered, modified, and deleted.

We will therefore need the management of the users who will work on the data and who will access the back office area, through username and password: the login process.

The "public" website of this application will display the objects divided by category and maybe some presentation pages of the customers' company.

<!=== Andrea Mauro Raimondi ===>

PRACTICE

At the following web addresses, you can see the final result of what we will build in the first part of this book.

http://www.aredit.com/public/PHPcourse/catalog/public/

http://www.aredit.com/public/PHPcourse/catalog/admin/

These simple pages will serve us to introduce the main concepts for the construction of a web application and the various languages used, HTML and PHP.

In the second part, we will see how to update the graphics of the application, and how the same data will appear different, by modifying the website's HTML, using a free HTML template.

Let's start by seeing what the home page of our project looks like.

Let's see what that result produced in the browser: an HTML file, obtained from the processing of PHP files by the webserver. Here is the code for the home page of the public website of our products catalog of which we have seen the image before.

```
<!doctype html public "-//w3c//dtd html 4.01 transitional//en"
        "http://www.w3.org/tr/html4/loose.dtd">
<html>
<head>
<title>...::: MY COMPANY - Catalogo prodotti :::...</title>
<meta http-equiv="Content-type" content="text/html; charset=iso-8859-1">
<meta name="author" content="Andrea Raimondi – info—AT--aredit.com">
<meta name="editor" content="Andrea Raimondi">
<meta name="robots" content="noindex">
<link rel="shortcut icon" href="../img/favicon.ico" />
<link rel=StyleSheet href="../css/73160000.css" type="text/css"
media=screen>
<style type="text/css">
a:link { color: #ff0000; }
a:active { color: #FFCC00; }
a:visited { color: #FF0000; }
</style>
</head>
<body>
<center>
<table border=1 cellpadding=0 cellspacing=0 bgcolor="#ffffff">
<tr>
<td>
<table cellspacing=0 cellpadding=0 border=0 width="760"
bgcolor="#9999cc">
    <tr>
    <td valign=top><img src="../img/php.gif" border=0
align=absmiddle></td>
    <td valign=top align=center><h1>MYPHP COMPANY</h1></td>
    <td valign=top align=right><img src="../img/php.gif" border=0
align=absmiddle></td>
```

<!=== Andrea Mauro Raimondi ===>

```
        </tr>
<tr bgcolor="#333366"><td colspan="3" height=10> </td></tr>
</table>
<table cellspacing=0 cellpadding=0 border=0 width="100%">
<tr>
<td valign=top align=center height=400>
<table>
<tr>
<td><a href="./">[ home ]</a></td>
<td><a href="categorie.php">[ categorie ]</a></td>
</tr>
</table>
<br><br><br>Benvenuti!
</td>
</tr>
</table>
</td><!-- tabella principale -->
</tr>
<tr>
<td valign=bottom>
<table cellspacing=0 cellpadding=0 border=0 width="100%"
bgcolor="#9999cc">
    <tr>
    <td align=center colspan=3>&copy; aredit.com</td>
    </tr>
</table>
</td>
</tr>
</table>
</center>
</body>
</html>
```

<?php Building Real World PHP Applications ?>

Each TAG is composed of an opening and a closing tag: let's take the <a> tag that defines a link: it looks like this

<a href="http://www.aredit.com"> Clickable text </ a>

the TAG is <a> which stands for an anchor; *href* is an attribute of the <a> tag; the text inside the opening and closing tags are affected by the behavior of the tag itself. In this case, the text, when the mouse moves over it, will highlight the fact that it represents a link to another web page. The *href* attribute determines which page will be reached once the text is clicked. Not all tags have the-closing tags, such as <meta> tags. In any case, remember that usually, a tag has its closing counterpart.

Perhaps now it is evident how an HTML TAG has constructed: one or more characters enclosed between the symbol <and the symbol>. The closing tag is represented by inserting a slash / between the <> symbols.

If a TAG has more than one *attribute*, these are inserted one after the other. Let's take the *table* tag you find in the home page code as an example.

<table cellspacing = "0" cellpadding = "0" border = 0 width = "100%" bgcolor = "# 9999cc">

You see five attributes. The syntax is as follows: attribute_name = "value". That is, after the name of the attribute, its value (which is variable according to needs) is placed in double quotation marks. In the case of the table tag, the attributes you see determine how it will be displayed on the screen, its width, the background color (bgcolor), if a border is to be displayed, the space between its cells (cellspacing) and the space inside its cells (cellpadding).

<!=== Andrea Mauro Raimondi ===>

The colors in HTML are in hexadecimal RGB (Red, Green, and Blue) format, a notation for which each color is given by the gradation of red, green, and blue. Each color is given by a pair of values. Values range from 00, absence of the base color, to FF, full color. So if I wanted to indicate the color red to the maximum degree, I would write #ff0000. If I wanted a gray I would write #cccccc;

Let's first see the generic structure of an HTML page and then analyze what we see on our home page.

Each html page begins with the document type declaration

<! doctype html public "- // w3c // dtd html 4.01 transitional // en" "http://www.w3.org/tr/html4/loose.dtd">

or

<! DOCTYPE html>

In which the browser understand that it must treat the document that arrives from the server as HTML. It has a series of attributes such as the reference standard the HTML is a subset of an XML document with the specifications that define it.

Each html file must have a <html> </html> tag.

Inside, the <head> </head> and <body> tags are inserted </body>; generating the following structure:

<html>
<head></head>
<body>
</body>
</html>

In the <head> tag you insert generic information about the file, such as the title, through the <title> </title> tag, the meta tags and any css commands and javascript functions, which are valid for the whole document. We will see later what css and javascript are used for. From our example, between the <head> </head> tags we find

<link rel=StyleSheet href="../css/73160000.css" type="text/css" media=screen>

inclusion of an external css file.

<meta http-equiv="Content-type" content="text/html; charset=iso-8859-1">
<meta name="author" content="Andrea Raimondi - info--AT--alchemist.it">

Meta tags that respectively define the character set to be used by the browser and the author of the html page.

The <body> and </body> tags contain the actual page that will be displayed in the browser. That is, it contains other tags that will serve to place text and images in the browser window.

For example inside the <body> tags are the <a> tags we saw earlier.

Tags are said to be *nested* when a tag such as the <body> tag contains other tags.

In our home we find the <img> tag

<img src="../img/php.gif" border=0 align=absmiddle>

With this tag, images are inserted into a web page. The main attribute is *src* which tells the server where to find the image, that is, the path within the folders that make up the site where we have saved the image. The path can be *"absolute"*, when a web URL is indicated, usually located outside our site; or *"relative"* when re-

<!=== Andrea Mauro Raimondi ===>

ferring to a folder that the server will search for starting from the Html page that contains it. In this case, the image is located in the folder we called "*img*" located outside the folder where the *index.php* file that represents our home is located.

In our application, we plan to use the following folders: *admin, public, css and img*. The *admin* folder will contain all the files that compose the back office area. The *public* folder will contain the actual site files. The *img* folder will contain the images we will use and the *css* folder the css files, we study it later. Clearly, each folder can contain all the folders that we eventually need.

Let's continue with the analysis of the *index.php* file that represents our public home.

Another key tag for building a web page is the <a> tag. The text and image enclosed between its opening and the closing tag </a> are made clickable. The main attribute of <a> is "*href*" which indicates the page to reach once the link is clicked. Another attribute that is often used is "*target*" which tells the browser where to open the page called by the link. It can be a new browser window (or new tab), if its value is "*_blank*". *<a href="categories.php"> [categories] </a>*. In this example, clicking "*categories*" will open the *categories.php* page. Having not specified a target, the link will open in the main browser window.

The tag that is used most on our sample site is the *<table>* tag. It creates a table, consisting of at least one row and one column. <Table> necessarily contains the <tr></tr> tags, which define a row, and the <td></td> tags which defines a column and its contents. Each of the tags that form a table has attributes. In the home

<?php Building Real World PHP Applications ?>

page, we have a <table> that defines and contains the header of the site

```
<table      cellspacing=0      cellpadding=0      border=0      width="760"
bgcolor="#9999cc">
    <tr>
    <td valign=top><img src="../img/php.gif" border=0
align=absmiddle></td>
        <td valign=top align=center><h1>MYPHP COMPANY</h1></td>
        <td valign=top align=right><img src="../img/php.gif" border=0
align=absmiddle></td>
    </tr>
<tr bgcolor="#333366"><td colspan="3" height=10> </td></tr>
</table>
```

We previously described the attributes of <table>, which can also be of <tr> and <td>.

If you look at the *index.php* HTML we notice that the page structure includes a main table consisting of two rows (two <tr>) each of which contains a column, a <td>. Inside the <td> other tables are nested, other <table> tags.

The use of the <table> tag for the structure of web pages was mainly used a few years ago because it allowed relatively precise positioning of an element on a web page. With the development of browsers and the speed of data lines and the development of the internet for mobile, the possibilities for web developers have increased and consequently, the types of tags available have increased. There are many innovations introduced with version 5 of the HTML language. To make a page displayed in the most optimized way for the diversity of devices currently in use, the latest versions of CSS and javascript libraries, such as JQuery, are used.

<!=== **Andrea Mauro Raimondi** ===>

The so-called web 2.0 is nothing more than the integration between HTML, CSS and javascript, optimized to improve the user experience for the same website on different devices, and the construction of the page structure has consequently undergone many changes. We will see this evolution in more detail in the second part of this book.

We find, again in the *index.php* file, three other tags, which are widely used: the <h1> </h1> tags, the <br> tag and the <center> </center> tags. The latter allows you to center everything it contains in available space. The tag <br> represents a line break: everything that follows it will be placed by the browser on a new line, that is, under the content that precedes it. The <h1> tag represents a way to format the text. It represents the header or title or subtitle of a block of text or a paragraph. The enclosed text is highlighted, increasing the font size compared to the one used in "normal" text. It can be modified through appropriate commands with style sheets, CSS. Other title tags are <h2></h2> <h3> </h3> until you get to <h6> </h6>, where the text is highlighted but in smaller size than <h1>.

The tag that creates a paragraph is <p> </p>

Other tags that are usually used for text formatting are:

<b></b> - Bold text
<strong> </strong> - Important text
<i> </i>- Italic text
<em> </em>- Emphasized text
<mark> </mark>- Marked text
<small> </small>- Smaller text

<?php Building Real World PHP Applications ?>

<del> </del>- Deleted text
<ins> </ins>- Inserted text
- Subscript text
- Superscript text

```
<!DOCTYPE html>
<html>
<body>

<p><b>1. This text is bold</b></p>

<p><i>2. This text is italic</i></p>

<p>3. This is<sub> subscript</sub> and <sup>superscript</sup></p>

<small>4. This is some smaller text.</small>

<p>5. Do not forget to buy <mark>milk</mark> today.</p>

<p>6. My favorite color is <del>blue</del> red.</p>

<p>7. My favorite color is <del>blue</del> <ins>red</ins>.</p>

</body>
</html>
```

1. This text is bold

2. This text is italic

3. This is $_{subscript}$ and ^{superscript}

4. This is some smaller text.

5. Do not forget to buy milk today.

6. My favorite color is ~~blue~~ red.

7. My favorite color is ~~blue~~ red.

There are also some tags to insert quotations into the text:

<abbr>   Defines an abbreviation or acronym
<address>   Defines contact information for the author/owner of a document
<bdo> Defines the text direction
<blockquote> Defines a section that is quoted from another source
<cite> Defines the title of a work
<q>   Defines a short inline quotation, inserisce delle virgolette
They all have their own closing tag.

<!=== Andrea Mauro Raimondi ===>

Another fundamental element to know concerns how comments are inserted in an HTML page. You see it in the index.php file:

<! - main table -- >

As can be guessed, the text that acts as a comment is enclosed between <! - and -->. And it is not displayed by the browser on the web page. They are seen only if we look directly into the page source from the browser.

<?php Building Real World PHP Applications ?>

In depth. Color management.

HTML colors are specified with predefined color names or with RGB, HEX, HSL, RGBA, or HSLA values

Below is an example using the color name:

<h1 bgcolor = "green"> Green </h1>

<h1 style = "background-color: orange;"> Orange </h1>

Or through the relative RGB code

<h1 style = "background-color: # ff6347;"> ... </h1>

<h1 bgcolor = "# 00FF00> Green </h1>

<h1 bgcolor = "# FFA500> Orange </h1>

As we have seen, with the *bgcolor* attribute we can set the **background** color of an html element:

<p bgcolor = "# ff0000"> </p>.

Or the text color: <p style = "color: Blue;"> Text blue </p>

Or the color of the border:

<h1 style = "border: 2px solid Violet;"> h1 with 2 pixel purple border </h1>

<!=== Andrea Mauro Raimondi ===>

In depth. The *style* attribute

The HTML *style* attribute is used to add styles to an element.

Major styles apply to an element's background color

<p style = "background-color: tomato;"> This is a paragraph. </p>

To the color of the text with the *color* attribute:

<p style = "color: red;"> Paragraph text is red </p>

It is used to change the type of font used, *font-family*:

<p style = "font-family: courier;"> This is a paragraph. </p>

The size of the text with *font-size*:

<p style = "font-size: 160%;"> This is a paragraph. </p>

The alignment of the text with *text-align*

<p style = "text-align: center;"> Centered paragraph. </p>

They all come from CSS commands, which we will see later.

```
<!DOCTYPE html>
<html>
<body style="background-color:lightgreen;">

<h1 style="text-align:center;">Titolo centrato</h1>
<p>Testo normale</p>
<p style="color:red;">Testo rosso</p>
<p style="color:blue;">Testo blue</p>
<p style="font-family:courier;font-size:120%;"><b>Paragrafo scritto
courier</b></p>
<p style="font-size:50px;">Testo grande</p>
<h1 style="background-color:powderblue;">Titolo con sfondo</h1>

</body>
</html>
```

Titolo centrato

Testo normale

Testo rosso

Testo blue

Paragrafo scritto courier

Testo grande

Titolo con sfondo

In Depth. Images

Images are embedded in an html page by means of the <img> tag. This tag has no closing tag.

<img **src** = "img_chania.jpg" **alt** = "Flowers in Chania" **width** = "460" **height** = "345">
It has two mandatory attributes *src* and *alt*. The first tells the browser where the image to be displayed is located on the server or on the internet. The *alt* attribute indicates the descriptive text of the image and appears if it is not displayed.

Other useful attributes are *width* and *height* which indicate the size in pixel of the image. We can also use *style*

 <img src = "img_girl.jpg" alt = "Girl in a jacket" **style** = "width: 500px; height: 600px;">

Below is the insertion of an image taken from a website, in this case the *src* attribute must have the absolute path.

```
<!DOCTYPE html>
<html>
<body>

<h2>HTML Image</h2>
<img src="http://www.fitnessedintorni.it/web/wp-content/uploads/2020/12
/Istantanea_2020-12-30_09-44-39.png" alt="Trulli" width="300" height="400">

</body>
</html>
```

HTML Image

<!=== Andrea Mauro Raimondi ===>

In Depth. Links

The creation of links, hyperlinks to another web page takes place with the <a> </a> tag. It can contain both text and images.

Links can also be made via the <button> tag. Here is an example <button onclick="document.location.href= 'default.asp'"> HTML Tutorial </button>

We have already seen the *href* and *target* attributes of <a>.

With the following command we can tell the browser to open the default mail program to send an email:

<a href="***mailto***:test@example.com"> Send email </a>

Another useful attribute of <a> is *title* which allows us to provide additional information with respect to the link, the title text appears above the mouse when it stops on the link, as in the following example:

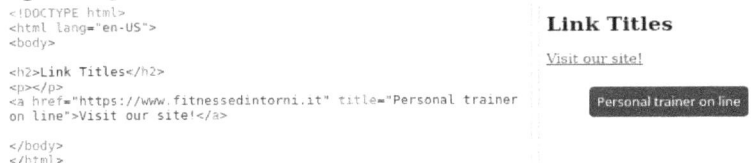

<?php Building Real World PHP Applications ?>

In Depth. Lists

HTML has the ability to create both numerically ordered and unordered lists.

```
<!DOCTYPE html>
<html>
<body>

<h2>An Unordered HTML List</h2>

<ul>
  <li>Book</li>
  <li>Pen</li>
  <li>Table</li>
</ul>

<h2>An Ordered HTML List</h2>

<ol>
  <li>Book</li>
  <li>Pen</li>
  <li>Table</li>
</ol>

</body>
</html>
```

An Unordered HTML List

- Book
- Pen
- Table

An Ordered HTML List

1. Book
2. Pen
3. Table

As you can see the tag that defines an ordered list is <ol> </ol>, each element of the list must be enclosed in the <li> </li> tag. The tag for the unordered list is <ul> </ul>, again the elements must be enclosed in the <li> </li> tag.

<!=== Andrea Mauro Raimondi ===>

In Depth. CSS

At this point we have seen the main HTML tags, we still have to see the tags for the construction of forms, a fundamental element of any web application because they allow interaction with the user and data manipulation. We will see them when we build the back office area for our project.

Let's take a closer look at CSS, which allows for the modification of some characteristics of the formatting tags.

CSS stands for *Cascading Style Sheets*.

With CSS you can control the layout of multiple web pages at the same time, managing the color, font, text size, spacing between elements, how elements are positioned and arranged, such as background images or colors of background need to be used, we can also use different layouts for different devices and screen sizes.

The word *cascade* means that a style applied to a parent element will also apply to all child elements within the parent. So if you set the text color of <body> to "blue", all headings, paragraphs, and other text elements within <body> will also have the same color, unless you apply a color different to a given element.

CSS can be added to HTML documents in 3 ways:

Inline: Using the style attribute within HTML elements

Internal: using a <style> element in the <head> section

External: Using a <link> element to link to an external CSS file

The most common way to add CSS is to keep styles in external CSS files.

Example of **inline** CSS i.e. applied directly inside a Tag

A red paragraph.

Example of **internal** CSS, inside a HTML file:

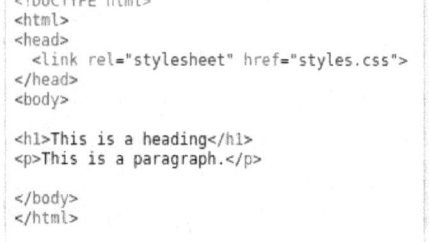

```
<!DOCTYPE html>
<html>
<head>
<style>
body {background-color: #cccccc;}
h1   {color: blue;}
p    {color: red;}
</style>
</head>
<body>

<h1>This is a heading</h1>
<p>This is a paragraph.</p>

</body>
</html>
```

Example of e**xternal** CSS, a standalone .css file

```
<!DOCTYPE html>
<html>
<head>
  <link rel="stylesheet" href="styles.css">
</head>
<body>

<h1>This is a heading</h1>
<p>This is a paragraph.</p>

</body>
</html>
```

<!=== Andrea Mauro Raimondi ===>

the *style.css* file, located in the same folder as the HTML file you see, contains the following text:

```
body {
 background-color: powderblue;
 font-family: verdana;
}
h1 {
 color: blue;
 font-size: 300%
}
p {
 color: red;
 border: 2px solid grey;
 margin: 50px;
}
```

With **external** CSS you can change the appearance of many pages at the same time by changing the content of a single .css file: all pages that include it through **<link>** will be affected by its formatting. In the .css file we are looking at, all tags of type <body><h1> <p> are directly affected. Through the use of *classes* by applying the ***class*** attribute, it is possible to format each single tag in a different way. For example, we will have <p> tags that behave in one way and others <p> that will behave in a different way.

```
<!DOCTYPE html>
<html>
<head>
<style>
.note {
  font-size: 170%;
  color: red;
}
</style>
</head>
<body>

<h1>My <span class="note">Important</span> Heading</h1>
<p>This is some <span class="note">important</span> text.</p>

</body>
</html>
```

My Important Heading

This is some important text.

<?php Building Real World PHP Applications ?>

CREATION OF MYSQL DATABASE

We will use MySQL as a database, one of the most used for web applications. MySQL is a *relational database* server.
Relational databases are systems for storing and accessing complex information. Major databases use **Structured Query Language (SQL)**, MySQL also uses SQL syntax for its interactions.
They are relational because they relate the tables to each other through the values of some fields. The *standardization* principle is used in the creation of the tables.
There are three main "*forms of normalization*".
Based on the **first normal form**, the data must be in a table structure and must meet the following criteria:
- each column must contain an "atomic" value, ie only one value per cell, so they must not be arrays
- each column must have a unique name
- each table must have one or more fields that uniquely identify the individual rows, must have at least one primary key
- two lines cannot be identical
- repeated groups of data are not allowed
below is an example that will clarify the concept expressed.

<!=== **Andrea Mauro Raimondi** ===>

Tabella problematica: Tabella Contatti

Idcontatto	Rag-sociale	Indirizzoazienda	Nomecontatto	Mansione	Tel	Email
1	Fiat	Via Verdi, Torino	Paolo Rossi	Presidente	34234	rossi@fiat.it
2	Fiat	Via Verdi, Torino	Giuseppe Verdi	Vice Presede	23423	verdi@fiat.it
3	Ford	Via Rossi, Monaco	Giacomo Puccini	Presidente	23423	puccini@ford.it

In the table, there are **repeated data** in the *Company name* and *Company address* columns. To normalize this table it is necessary to create a new "Companies" table which will contain the data relating to the single company. The *unique identifiers* (the primary key) of the Companies table will appear in the *Contacts* table:

Idcontatto	Idazienda	Nomecontatto	Mansione	Tel	Email
1	1	Paolo Rossi	Presidente	34234	rossi@fiat.it
2	1	Giuseppe Verdi	Vice Presede	23423	verdi@fiat.it
3	2	Giacomo Puccini	Presidente	23423	puccini@ford.it

Tabella Aziende

Idazienda	Ragionesociale	Indirizzoazienda
1	Fiat	Via Verdi, Torino
2	Ford	Via Rossi, Monaco

The **primary key** is a column or set of columns by which each row can be uniquely identified
It can be a primary key, for example, a column with a *sequential value*. In MySQL there are *auto_increment fields* that insert a unique sequential number each time a record is added. Primary key can be emails, URLs, social security numbers or other elements that by their nature are unique.

<?php Building Real World PHP Applications ?>

The **second normal form** applies to tables that have more than one primary key.

Idazienda	Ragionesociale	Indirizzoazienda	Cittaazienda	Presidente
1	Fiat	Via Verdi, 55	Torino	Giuseppe Verdi
2	Ford	Via Rossi, 15	Monaco	Antonio Vivaldi

In this table, there are two primary keys: Company Account and Company City. The problem arises when another address is entered for the Fiat company: the name of the president *is repeated*. Rows that are only partially dependent on the primary key must be removed and inserted into a new Address table

In the **third normal form**, all fields must describe the primary key and therefore must describe the function of the table, in this case, we have a *Contacts* table:

Idcontatto	Nomecontatto	Mansione	Tel	Email	SegretarioCont	Tel-segretario
1	Paolo Rossi	Presidente	34234	rossi@fiat.it	Luigi Cherubini	12345
2	Giuseppe Verdi	Vice Presede	23423	verdi@fiat.it	Vincenzo Bellini	678900
3	Giacomo Puccini	Presidente	23423	puccini@ford.it	Arcangelo Corelli	1479765

The Tel-secretary field does not describe the primary key (a contact) and must be placed in another table (a Secretaries table).
Tables can have *different types of relationships* with each other.
One-to-many relationship: a value in a column refers to different fields of another table, for example, the sectors table with the companies table, as seen in the following diagram.
One-to-one relationship: a special case of a one-to-many relationship, in which a column of a table refers to a field in another table, such as the manager's table with the assistant's table.

<!=== Andrea Mauro Raimondi ===>

Many-to-many relationship: different fields in a table refer to some fields in another table, for example, the newsletter table and the subscriber's table, generate the fields of the newsletter subscribers table.

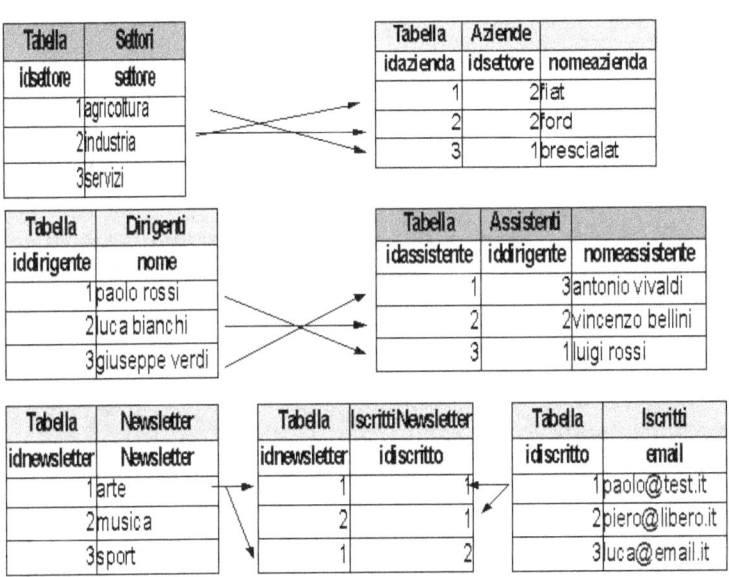

Tabella	Settori
idsettore	settore
1	agricoltura
2	industria
3	servizi

Tabella	Aziende	
idazienda	idsettore	nomeazienda
1	2	fiat
2	2	ford
3	1	brescialat

Tabella	Dirigenti
iddirigente	nome
1	paolo rossi
2	luca bianchi
3	giuseppe verdi

Tabella	Assistenti	
idassistente	iddirigente	nomeassistente
1	3	antonio vivaldi
2	2	vincenzo bellini
3	1	luigi rossi

Tabella	Newsletter
idnewsletter	Newsletter
1	arte
2	musica
3	sport

Tabella	IscrittiNewsletter	
idnewsletter	idiscritto	
1	1	
2	1	
1	2	

Tabella	Iscritti
idiscritto	email
1	paolo@test.it
2	piero@libero.it
3	luca@email.it

For the creation of databases and tables, we use the phpMyAdmin tool. PhpMyAdmin is itself a web application written in PHP, the first version dates back to 1998. It can be downloaded from *https://www.phpmyadmin.net*

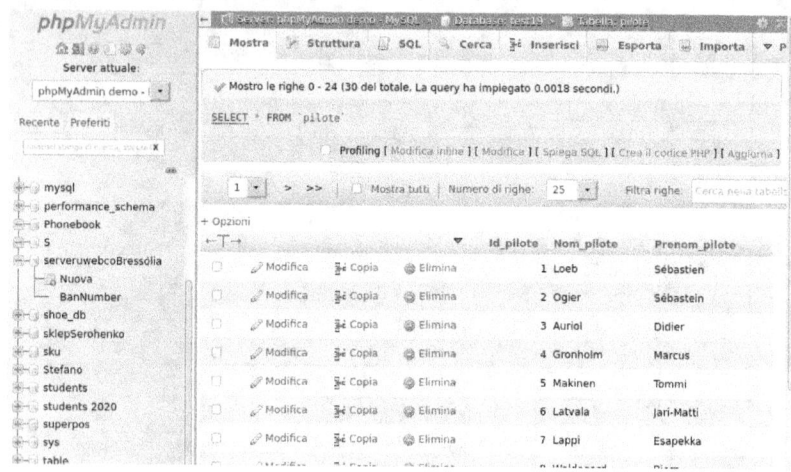

Through phpMyAdmin, we create the tables of a database using the SQL language. In our application we will need the following tables: *users* with whom we will manage the users who can access the application management back office; *logutenti_admin*, which is the table we will use to keep track of accesses and for session checks; *categories* with which we will manage the product categories and the *product* table that will contain the product data.

<!=== Andrea Mauro Raimondi ===>

Below is the SQL syntax for creating tables.
CREATE TABLE `PHP_course_users` (
  `iduser` int(4) NOT NULL auto_increment,
  `name` varchar(250) NOT NULL default '',
  `username` varchar(50) NOT NULL default '',
  `password` varchar(50) NOT NULL default '',
  `active` int(2) NOT NULL default '0',
  `level` int(2) NOT NULL default '1',
  `lastaccess` datetime NOT NULL default '0000-00-00 00:00:00',
  `naccess` int(4) NOT NULL default '0',
  PRIMARY KEY (`iduser`)
) TYPE=MyISAM ;

CREATE TABLE `PHP_course_logutenti_admin` (
  `IDLOG` int(4) NOT NULL auto_increment,
  `IDUTENTE` mediumint(4) default NULL,
  `SESSIONID` varchar(50) default NULL,
  `STATE` int(4) default NULL,
  `CREATIONDATE` datetime default '0000-00-00 00:00:00',
  `DATALOGOUT` datetime default NULL,
  `IP` varchar(20) default NULL,
  `URL` varchar(255) default NULL,
  PRIMARY KEY (`IDLOG`)
) TYPE=MyISAM ;

CREATE TABLE `PHP_course_categories` (
  `idcategory` int(11) NOT NULL auto_increment,
  `category` varchar(250) NOT NULL default '',
  PRIMARY KEY (`idcategory`),
  KEY `category` (`category`)
) TYPE=MyISAM ;

```
CREATE TABLE `PHP_course_products` (
 `idproduct` int(4) NOT NULL auto_increment,
 `idcategory` int(4) NOT NULL default '0',
 `product_name` varchar(255) NOT NULL default '',
 `description` text NOT NULL,
 `quantity` int(4) NOT NULL default '0',
 `price` decimal(10,2) NOT NULL default '0.00',
 `tax` int(2) NOT NULL default '0',
 `img` varchar(250) NOT NULL default '',
 PRIMARY KEY (`idproduct`)
) ENGINE=MyISAM  DEFAULT CHARSET=latin1;
```

From these simple tables we can see the types of data we will be using. **Data types** identify what a given field contains. They can be text strings, numbers, dates. Each type contains different categories based on the memory that is used to store the data. All types of columns can contain (if declared in their definition) the **NULL** value, required by the SQL standard to indicate a "non-value", ie the fact that a certain column may not have a value on some rows of the table.

<!=== Andrea Mauro Raimondi ===>

MySQL DATA TYPE: NUMBERS

TINYINT[(M)]
SMALLINT[(M)]
MEDIUMINT[(M)]
INT[(M)]
BIGINT[(M)]
FLOAT[(M,D)]
DOUBLE[(M,D)]
DECIMAL[(M[,D])]

The data of type **TINYINT**, **SMALLINT**, **MEDIUMINT**, **INT** and **BIGINT** represent integers composed respectively of 1, 2, 3, 4 and 8 bytes. The TINYINT can contain 256 values, ranging from -128 to +127 or from 0 to 255 in the case of UNSIGNED. Likewise, SMALLINT can hold 65536 values, MEDIUMINT 16,777,216, INT over 4 billion, BIGINT about 18 billion billion.
The indication of the **M** parameter on the integers does not affect the values that can be stored, but represents the minimum length that can be displayed for the data. If the value takes up fewer digits, it is filled on the left with spaces, or with zeros if the ZERO-FILL option is added.

FLOAT and **DOUBLE** represent floating point numbers. M represents the total number of digits represented and D the number of decimal digits.

FLOAT is "single precision": its theoretical limits range from -3.402823466E+ 38 to -1.175494351E-38 and from 1.175494351E-38 to 3.402823466E+38, in addition to zero.

The **DOUBLE** values are "double precision": the theoretical limits are from -1.7976931348623157E + 308 to -2.2250738585072014E-308 and from 2.2250738585072014E-308 to 1.7976931348623157E + 308, in addition to zero.

Finally, the **DECIMAL** data represent "exact" numbers, with M total digits of which D decimals. The default values are 10 for M and 0 for D. The limit values for this data are the same as for DOUBLE. The maximum allowed digits is 65 for M and 30 for D. Starting with MySQL 5.0.3 this data is compressed in binary form.

<!=== Andrea Mauro Raimondi ===>

MySQL DATA TYPE: DATE AND TIME

The date and time columns are as follows:
AT YOUR PLACE
DATETIME
TIMESTAMP [(M)]
TIME
YEAR [(2 | 4)]

A **DATE** column can contain dates from '1000-01-01' (1th January 1000) to '9999-12-31' (31 December 9999). MySQL displays the dates in the format we just showed you, but allows you to enter them in the form of strings or numbers.

A **DATETIME** column contains a date and time, with the same range seen for DATE. The display is in the format 'YYYY-MM-DD HH: MM: SS', but also in this case different formats can be used for the insertion.

The values corresponding to the Unix timestamp can be stored in a **TIMESTAMP**, ranging from midnight on January 1, 1970 to an unspecified time in the year 2037.

A **TIME** column contains a time value (hours, minutes and seconds) ranging from '-838: 59: 59' to '838: 59: 59'. Here, too, the display takes place in the indicated format, but it is possible to use different formats for insertion.

Finally, the **YEAR** column represents, on four digits, a year between 1901 and 2155, or 0000. On two digits, on the other hand, the values range from 70 (1970) to 69 (2069).

<?php Building Real World PHP Applications ?>

MySQL DATA TYPE: STRING

[NATIONAL] CHAR(M) [BINARY | ASCII | UNICODE]
[NATIONAL] VARCHAR(M) [BINARY]
BINARY(M)
VARBINARY(M)
TINYBLOB
TINYTEXT
BLOB[(M)]
TEXT[(M)]
MEDIUMBLOB
MEDIUMTEXT
LONGBLOB
LONGTEXT
ENUM('value 1','value 2',…)
SET('value 1','value 2',…)
In square brackets the optional parameters.

CHAR is a fixed-length string (M) padded with spaces to the right at the time of storage, which are discarded on reading. The expected length is from 0 to 255 characters. The NATIONAL option indicates that the string must use the default character set. The **BINARY** attribute indicates that the binary collation of the character set used must be used. ASCII assigns the character set latin1, UNICODE assigns ucs2.
CHAR BYTE is equivalent to **CHAR BINARY**. Note that if a row has variable length (ie if at least one column is defined as va-

<!=== Andrea Mauro Raimondi ===>

riable length) any CHAR field longer than 3 characters is converted to VARCHAR.

VARCHAR is a variable-length string; its characteristics have changed since MySQL 5.0.3: previously, in fact, the maximum length was 255 and the empty spaces on the right were eliminated during storage; but now this is no longer the case and the maximum declarable length has risen to 65535 characters. The NATIONAL and BINARY attributes have the same meaning as seen in CHAR. If you define a VARCHAR column with less than 4 characters it will be transformed into CHAR.

BINARY and **VARBINARY** match CHAR and VARCHAR, but store strings of bytes instead of characters. They therefore have no character sets. BINARY values receive a right padding of 0x00 bytes starting with MySQL 5.0.15; previously the padding was whitespace and was removed on reading.

The formats of type BLOB and TEXT are used for binary and text values respectively.

The maximum length is 255 characters for TINYBLOB and TINYTEXT, 65535 for BLOB and TEXT, 16,777,215 for MEDIUMBLOB and MEDIUMTEXT, 4 gigabytes for LONGBLOB and LONGTEXT.

An **ENUM** column can contain one of the values listed in the definition, or NULL or an empty string, which is assigned when trying to enter an invalid value. Possible values can be up to 65535.

<?php Building Real World PHP Applications ?>

A **SET** column, like the ENUM, provides a set of possible values
(up to 64), but in this case the column can have more than one value, or none.

idproduct	int(4)
idcategory	int(4)
product_name	varchar(255)
description	text
quantity	int(4)
price	decimal(10,2)
tax	int(2)
img	varchar(250)

<!=== Andrea Mauro Raimondi ===>

MYSQL INDEXES

PRIMARY KEY: applied to one or more fields of a table, it allows you to uniquely distinguish each row. The field subjected to the primary key index does not allow duplicates or null fields;
UNIQUE: similar to the primary key, with the difference that it tolerates null values, while duplicates are prohibited;
COLUMN INDEX: these are the most common indices. Applied to a field in a table, they are purely to speed up access by allowing duplicate and null values;
FULLTEXT: These are indexes that allow you to speed up time-consuming and memory-intensive operations, such as text search on an entire field.

The structure of the database we have created is now clearer.
PhpMyAdmin in *structure view*, shows the types of data and their characteristics as shown in the following image:

Campo	Tipo	Collation	Attributi	Null	Predefinito	Extra
idprodotto	int(4)			No		auto_increment
idcategoria	int(4)			No	0	
prodotto	varchar(255)	latin1_swedish_ci		No		
descrizione	text	latin1_swedish_ci		No		
quantitadisp	int(4)			No	0	
costo	decimal(10,2)			No	0.00	
iva	int(2)			No	0	

Seleziona tutti / Deseleziona tutti *Se selezionati:*

You can download the entire database in SQL format and import it directly into your own using the import function of phpMyAdmin. Write to info@aredit.com to request all the files.

<?php Building Real World PHP Applications ?>

<!=== Andrea Mauro Raimondi ===>

BUILDING THE BACK OFFICE AREA

We work now in the admin folder, in it, we have the following files:

For the webserver, the home page is index.php or index.html. This means that if you do not specify a particular page in a URL but only indicate a folder on a web server, the server will try to display the index.php or index.html page. Each web server can be specially set up to serve any type of file as the starting page.

In our case, the *index.php* page will refer to the *login.php* page: we are in a reserved area and we want to authenticate prior to access the contents of the folder and our application.

In the file that I report, I also left, as a curiosity, a possible alternative to redirect: the use of *framesets*. *Framesets* were used years ago to divide the display area into different areas, each of which displayed a different file, the different areas could interact with each other through javascript commands. Frames was used most when there were no javascript libraries, like JQuery, yet.

```php
1   <?php
2   //****************************************************
3   //AUTHOR: andrea raimondi info--AT--aredit.com
4   //file: frameset iniziale
5   //****************************************************
6
7   header("Location: login.php");
8   die();
9   ?>
10  <html>
11  <head>
12  <title>...::: MY COMPANY - Catalogo prodotti :::...</title>
13  <meta http-equiv="Content-type" content="text/html; charset=UTF-8">
14  <meta name="author" content="Andrea Raimondi info--AT--aredit.com">
15  <meta name="editor" content="Andrea Raimondi">
16  <link rel="shortcut icon" href="../img/favicon.ico" />
17  </head>
18  <frameset cols="0,*" frameborder="NO" border="0" framespacing="0" rows="*">
19    <frame name="menu" src="white.html">
20    <frame name="dx" scrolling="yes" noresize src="login.php">
21  </frameset>
22  <noframes>
23  <body bgcolor="#FFFFFF" text="#000000">
24    <p>
25    Your brower does not suppor frames!
26  </body>
27  </noframes>
28  </html>
```

To perform the redirect we use the PHP *header* function which simply contains the reference to the page to be recalled.

We immediately note that the code block in PHP language must be enclosed between the symbols **<?php and ?>**: Everything enclosed between these tags will be analyzed by the webserver through the PHP engine. After the header we find the function *die()* which simply ends the execution of the script. Looking at the php page we realize that it also contains HTML code. In fact, what is

<!=== Andrea Mauro Raimondi ===>

produced by a php page is HTML code, which is sent from the server to the browser to be displayed. So the php code processes the data and returns them, in our example, in HTML format.

This is the norm. With PHP we can generate other types of files, especially text files, such as .txt, csv, json, and others.

The php code block can also be inserted inside an html tag, to make its content dynamic. Here is an example of a background color:

```
<td bgcolor = <?php print $bgcolor;?> </td>
```

In this case the *$bgcolor* variable can assume different colors according to what is established by the program. **Variables** are "containers" for storing information. They are the basic element of any programming language. In PHP, a variable begins with a *$ sign*, followed by the variable name:

```
<?php
$txt = "Hello world!";
$x = 5;
$y = 10.5;
?>
```

After executing the above statements, the $txt variable will contain the value Hello world !, the $x variable will contain the value 5 and the $y variable will contain the value 10.5. When assigning a *text value* to a variable we need to enclose the value in quotation marks. Unlike other programming languages, PHP has no command to declare a variable. A variable is created when it is first assigned a value. Variables in PHP are *case-sensitive*, that is, the language discriminates between upper and lower case:

$NAME is a variable other than $name or $Name or even $nAmE.

Find more explanations in the PHP index at the end of the book.

When we reach the index.php page with the browser, we are immediately redirected to the login.php page which manages the authentication of the user enabled to access the back office area.

<!=== Andrea Mauro Raimondi ===>

The login.php page asks the visitor to enter username and password through two fields of an HTML form.

Here is the code that creates the form you see.

```
32    <form action="<?php print "login.php"; ?>" method="post">
33    <tr>
34            <td colspan=3 class="ss" align=center>INSERT USERNAME AND PASSWORD</td>
35    </tr>
36    <tr>
37            <td><img src="../img/trasp.gif" width=1 height=10></td>
38    </tr>
39    <tr>
40            <td align=center>
41                    <table border=0 cellspacing=0 cellpadding=0>
42                    <tr>
43                            <td>Username </td>
44                            <td><input type="text" name="userk" size="20"></td>
45                    </tr>
46                    <tr>
47                            <td>Password </td>
48                            <td><input type="password" name="passk" size="20"></td>
49                    </tr>
50                    </table>
51            </td>
52    </tr>
53    <tr>
54            <td><img src="../img/trasp.gif" width=1 height=10></td>
55    </tr>
56    <tr>|
57            <td colspan=3 align=center>
58                    <input type="submit" value="immetti">
59                    <input type="reset" value="annulla">
60            </td>
61    </tr>
62    </form>
```

We already know the <table> tag which is used to position the elements of a web page. HTML forms are included by the <form> </form> tag whose main attributes are *action*, which indicates where the form must transmit the data it contains, *method*, which indicates the data transmission mode: it can be GET or POST, and *name* indicating the name of the form, which will be used to identify it and manipulate its components, usually through javascript functions. Within that tag, the other tags display the different types of fields available. We see them in the in-depth analysis that follows.

<?php Building Real World PHP Applications ?>

In depth. HTML forms

An HTML form is used to collect user input. User input is often sent to a server for processing. It is created by inserting some tags inside the <form> </form> tag. As seen previously, the attributes of <form> are *action, method, name.* We also add the *target* attribute that specifies where to display the response that is received after submitting the form data. It can assume the following values *_blank,* in a new window or tab, *_self,* in the same window; *_parent* in a frame higher than the one containing the form. If you do not indicate the data will be displayed in the same window where the form exists.

The main elements and tags that can build a form are:

   <input>
   <label></label>
   <select></select>
   <option></option>
   <textarea></textarea>
   <button>

The <**input**> element is one of the most used for building a form and can be displayed in different ways based on the value of the type attribute.

The <**label**> tag defines a "label" referring to an element of the form through the *for* attribute, as in the following example:

<!=== Andrea Mauro Raimondi ===>

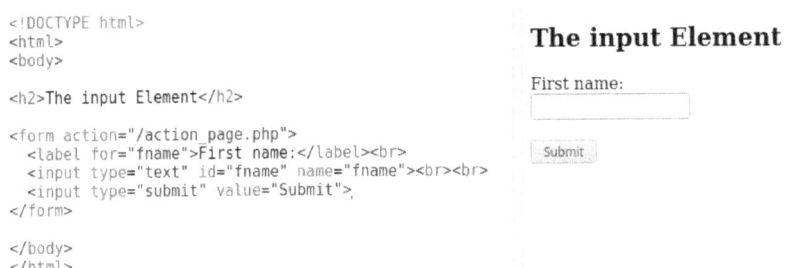

```
<!DOCTYPE html>
<html>
<body>

<h2>The input Element</h2>

<form action="/action_page.php">
  <label for="fname">First name:</label><br>
  <input type="text" id="fname" name="fname"><br><br>
  <input type="submit" value="Submit">
</form>

</body>
</html>
```

The for attribute of <label> refers to the value assumed by the *id* attribute of another element.

The <select> </select> element defines a drop-down list, its possible selectable options are indicated by the <option> </option> tag. The main attributes are *name* and *value*. The first defines a unique name for the form field and will be used to send the content of the field itself through the browser query string or within the browser *header* if the post is used as a method. In a nutshell, it represents the name of the variable. *Value* represents the content of that field and will contain what will be sent as a value relative to that field to the server.

```
<!DOCTYPE html>
<html>
<body>

<h2>The select Element</h2>

<p>The select element defines a drop-down list:</p>

<form action="/action_page.php">
  <label for="cars">Choose a car:</label>
  <select id="cars" name="cars">
    <option value="volvo">Volvo</option>
    <option value="saab">Saab</option>
    <option value="fiat">Fiat</option>
    <option value="audi">Audi</option>
  </select>
  <input type="submit">
</form>

</body>
</html>
```

The select Element

The select element defines a drop-down list:

Choose a car: Volvo ∨ Invia richiesta

The <textarea> </textarea> element defines a multiline text field. The *rows* attribute specifies the visible number of rows in a text area. The *cols* attribute specifies the visible width of a text area.

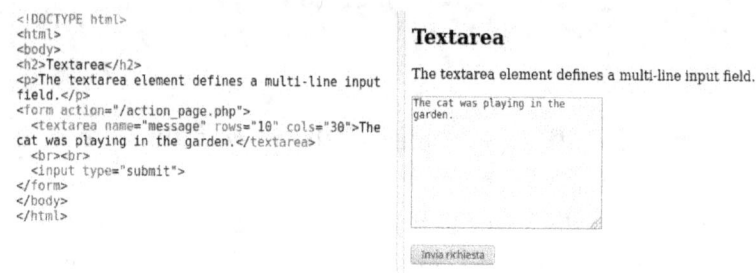

The <button> </button> form element defines a clickable button

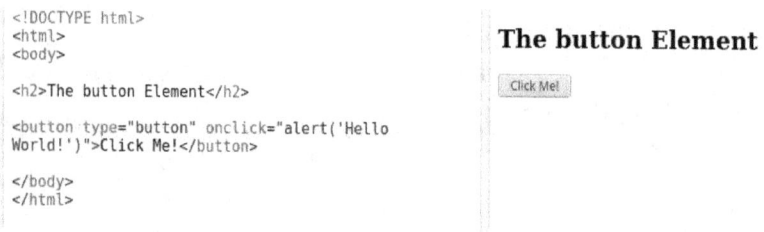

The <input type="button"> field can also be used for the same purpose, as we will see shortly.

<!=== Andrea Mauro Raimondi ===>

In Depth. <input *type*="...">
The <input> type field can have the following types, through the
value of its *type* attribute:
    <input type="button">
    <input type="checkbox">
    <input type="color">
    <input type="date">
    <input type="datetime-local">
    <input type="email">
    <input type="file">
    <input type="hidden">
    <input type="image">
    <input type="month">
    <input type="number">
    <input type="password">
    <input type="radio">
    <input type="range">
    <input type="reset">
    <input type="search">
    <input type="submit">
    <input type="tel">
    <input type="text">
    <input type="time">
    <input type="url">
    <input type="week">
Let's see in more detail the most used.

\<input type = "**text**"> defines a one-line text field
always indicate the name attribute for all \<input> tags
\<input type = "**password**"> defines a password field where what
you type is not displayed

```
<!DOCTYPE html>
<html>
<body>
<h2>Text and Password field</h2>
<p>The <strong>input type="password"</strong> defines a
password field:</p>
<form action="/action_page.php">
  <label for="username">Username:</label><br>
  <input type="text" id="username" name="username"><br>
  <label for="pwd">Password:</label><br>
  <input type="password" id="pwd" name="pwd"><br><br>
  <input type="submit" value="Submit">
</form>
<p>The characters in a password field are masked (shown as
asterisks or circles).</p>
</body>
</html>
```

Password field

The **input type="password"** defines a password field:

Username:
[dddd]
Password:
[••••]

[Submit]

The characters in a password field are masked (shown as asterisks or circles).

\<input type = "**submit**"> defines a button for submitting form data to a page that will handle the data (form-handler). This page is specified in the action attribute of the \<form> tag. The text that appears above the button is set through the value attribute.

\<input type = "**reset**"> defines a reset button which will reset all module values to their default values.

```
<!DOCTYPE html>
<html>
<body>

<h2>Submit and Reset Button</h2>

<form action="/action_page.php">
  <label for="fname">First name:</label><br>
  <input type="text" id="fname" name="fname" value="John"><br>
  <label for="lname">Last name:</label><br>
  <input type="text" id="lname" name="lname" value="Doe">
<br><br>
  <input type="submit" value="Send data">
  <input type="reset" value="Undo">
</form>

<p>If you change the input values and then click the "Reset"
button, <br>the form-data will be reset to the default
values.</p>

</body>
</html>
```

Submit and Reset Button

First name:
[John]
Last name:
[Doe]

[Send data] [Undo]

If you change the input values and then click the "Reset" button, the form-data will be reset to the default values.

<!=== Andrea Mauro Raimondi ===>

<input type = "**radio**"> defines a radio button.

Radio buttons allow a user to select **only one choice** from a limited number of them.

<input type = "**checkbox**"> defines a checkbox.

Checkboxes allow a user to select **zero** or **more options** from a limited number of choices.

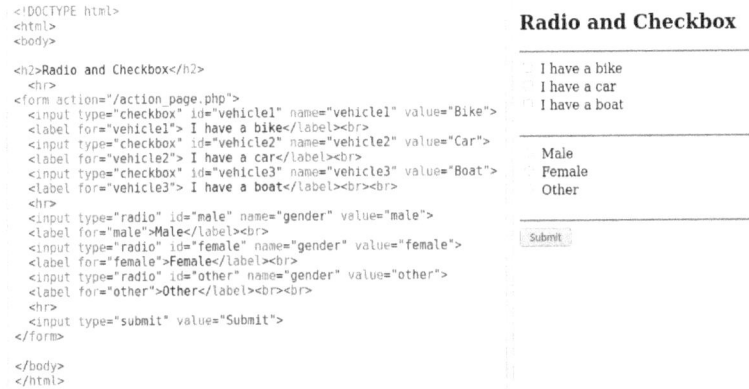

<input type = "**button**"> defines a button

<input type = "**color**"> is used for input fields which should contain a color. Depending on your browser support, a color picker may appear in the input field.

<input type = "**date**"> is used for input fields which should contain a date. Depending on your browser support, a date picker may appear in the input field. With the min and max attributes, you can add restrictions to dates.

<input type = "**email**"> is used for input fields which should contain an email address. Depending on the browser support, the email address can be automatically validated at the time of sen-

ding. Some smartphones recognize the email type and add ".com" to the keyboard to match the email input.

<input type = "**number**"> defines a numeric input field.

You can also set restrictions on accepted numbers. The following example shows a numeric input field, where you can enter a value between 1 and 5

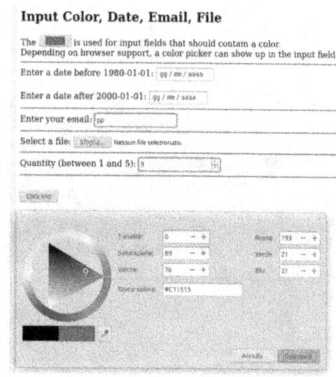

<input type = "**range**"> defines a control for entering a number whose exact value is not important (such as a slider control). The default range is 0 to 100. However, you can set restrictions on accepted numbers with the min, max, and step attributes:

<input type = "**search**"> is used for search fields (a search field behaves like a normal text field).

<input type = "**tel**"> is used for input fields which should contain a phone number.

<!=== Andrea Mauro Raimondi ===>

<input type = "**time**"> allows the user to select a time (no time zone). Depending on browser support, a time picker may appear in the input field.

<input type = "**url**"> is used for input fields which should contain a URL address. Depending on browser support, the URL field may be automatically validated when submitted. Some smartphones recognize the URL type and add ".com" to the keyboard to match the URL input.

```
<!DOCTYPE html>
<html>
<body>
<form action="/action_page.php">
<h3>Display a Range Input Field</h3>
  <label for="vol">Volume (between 0 and 50):</label>
  <input type="range" id="vol" name="vol" min="0" max="50">

<hr>
<h3>Display a  Search, Input Field</h3>
  <label for="gsearch">Search Google:</label>
  <input type="search" id="gsearch" name="gsearch">
<hr>
<h3>Display a Tel Input Field</h3>
  <label for="phone">Enter your phone number:</label>
  <input type="tel" id="phone" name="phone" pattern="[0-9]{3}-[0-9]{2}-[0-9]{3}">
<hr>
<h3>Display a Time Input Field</h3>
  <label for="appt">Select a time:</label>
  <input type="time" id="appt" name="appt">
<hr>
<h3>Display an  URL Input Field</h3>
  <label for="homepage">Add your homepage:</label>
  <input type="url" id="homepage" name="homepage"><hr>
  <br>
  <input type="submit" value="Submit">
</form>
</body>
</html>
```

This is what you see in the browser:

Display a Range Input Field

Volume (between 0 and 50): ════════○════════

Display a Search, Input Field

Search Google: [   ]

Display a Tel Input Field

Enter your phone number: [   ]

Display a Time Input Field

Select a time: [-- : --]

Display an URL Input Field

Add your homepage: [   ]

[Submit]

<!=== Andrea Mauro Raimondi ===>

In Depth. <input> attributes

The *value* attribute of <input> specifies an initial value for an input field.

The *read-only* attribute specifies that an input field is read-only. A read-only input field cannot be edited (however, a user can select it with the tab key, highlight it, and copy text from it). The value of a read-only input field will still be sent when you submit the form.

The *disabled* attribute specifies that an input field should be disabled. A disabled input field is unusable and not clickable. The value of a disabled input field will not be submitted when the form is submitted.

The *size* attribute specifies the visible width, in characters, of an input field. The default value for the size is 20. Note: The size attribute works with the following input types: text, submit, tel, url, email, and password.

The *maxlength* attribute specifies the maximum number of characters allowed in an input field.

The *min* and *max* attributes specify the minimum and maximum values for an input field. The min and max attributes work with the following input types: number, range, date, datetime-local, month, time. Tip: Use the max and min attributes together to create a range of allowed values.

The *multiple* attribute specifies that the user is allowed to enter more than one value in an input field. This attribute works with the following types of inputs: email and file.

The **pattern** attribute specifies a regular expression against which the value of the input field is checked when the form is submitted. The pattern attribute works with the following types of input: text, date, search, url, tel, email, and password.

The **placeholder** attribute specifies a brief hint that describes the expected value of an input field (a sample value or a brief description of the expected format). The short tip appears in the entry field before the user enters a value. The placeholder attribute works with the following types of input: text, search, url, tel, email, and password.

The **required** attribute specifies that an input field must be filled in before submitting the form. The required attribute works with the following types of inputs: text, search, url, tel, email, password, date pickers, number, checkbox, radio, and file.

The **step** attribute specifies the valid number ranges for an input field. Example: if step = "4", the legal numbers could be -4, 0, 4, 8, etc. This attribute can be used in conjunction with the max and min attributes to create a range of valid values. The step attribute works with the following types of input: number, range, date, time.

The **autofocus** attribute specifies that an input field should be activated automatically when the page is loaded.

The **height** and **width** attributes specify the height and width of an <input type = "image"> element

The **autocomplete** attribute specifies whether a form or input field should have autocomplete enabled or disabled. Autocomplete allows the browser to predict the value. When a user begins ty-

<!=== **Andrea Mauro Raimondi** ===>

ping in a field, the browser should display options for filling in the field, based on the values previously typed. The *autocomplete* attribute works with <form> and the following <input> types: text, search, url, tel, email, password, datepickers, range, and color.

An example:

```html
<!DOCTYPE html>
<html>
<body>
<form action="/action_page.php" autocomplete="on">
  <label for="fname">First name:</label>
  <input type="text" id="fname" name="fname" autofocus required><br><br>
  <label for="lname">Last name:</label>
  <input type="text" id="lname" name="lname"><br><br>
  <label for="email">Email:</label>
  <input type="email" id="email" name="email" autocomplete="off" required
placeholder="youremail@email.com"><br><br>
  <input type="submit" value="Submit">
</form>

</body>
</html>
```

First name: [   ]

Last name: [   ]

Email: [youremail@email.com]

[Submit]

LOGIN MANAGEMENT

After this brief overview of HTML forms and their main components, let's resume the analysis of the login.php file.

Once the login, username, and password have been entered, the user, by clicking on the submit button, will send the data to the page we have defined through the action attribute of the <form> tag. In our case it looks like this:

<form action = "<?php print " login.php"; ?>" method = "post">

Therefore the data will be sent to the same page (login.php), through the post method, that is, through the HTTP requests that the browser sends to the webserver. The page, as we see below, has a PHP code block that takes care of retrieving the HTML form data from the HTTP headers, performing some possible checks, and fi-

```
1   <?php
2   //********************************************************
3   //AUTHOR: andrea raimondi info--AT--aredit.com
4   //file:  login
5   //********************************************************
6   include('zz_top_inc.php');
7   ?>
8   <p>
9   <br><img src="../img/trasp.gif" width=1 height=20 alt="">
10  <table border=0 cellspacing=0 cellpadding=0>
11  <?php
12  //retrive and check form data
13  //recupero e controllo dati del form
14  $userk = $_REQUEST["userk"];
15  $passk = $_REQUEST["passk"];
16  if((isset($userk)) && (isset($passk))){
17  //trim
18  //tolgo eventuali spazi vuoti
19  $userk=trim($userk);
20  $passk=trim($passk);
21  //variabile con codice SQL
22  $sqlb = "SELECT * FROM PHP_course_users WHERE username='$userk' AND password='$passk' AND active='1'";
23  $resultb = mysqli_query($connection,$sqlb) or die(mysqli_error());
24  $exist = mysqli_num_rows($resultb);
25  if($exist<= 0) {
26  print "
27  <tr><td height=30 colspan=3 align=center>
28  <!--Forgot password? <a href=\"forgetpw.php\">click HERE</a>.-->
29  <br><img src=\"trasp.gif\" width=1 height=40 alt=\"\"></td></tr>
30  <tr><td height=30 colspan=3 align=center bgcolor=\"#ffff00\">Wrong User ID o password!<br>
31   </td></tr>";
32  ?>
33
34  <form action="<?php print "login.php"; ?>" method="post">
35  <tr>
36      <td colspan=3 class="ss" align=center>INSERT USERNAME AND PASSWORD</td>
37  </tr>
38  <tr>
39      <td><img src="../img/trasp.gif" width=1 height=10></td>
40  </tr>
```

<!=== Andrea Mauro Raimondi ===>

nally checking if the data sent corresponds to a user with access permissions to the system.

As you can see, the include() function is inserted in line 6, the purpose of which is to include another file within a PHP page. This is a very useful feature because it saves you from writing a lot of code, both HTML and PHP.

In our application, we find two files for both the back office area and the public site included in almost all the other pages: zz_top_inc.php and zz_bottom_inc.php. As their names may imply, they have the function, respectively, of creating the HTML and PHP code for the header of the pages and the footer (i.e. of the lower area) of the pages. This is for the simple reason that the code is the same for all files: the top part will contain, for example, the logo and the menu. The bottom part will contain other information that we believe is useful to be always present, such as, for example, telephone, email, and copyrights. We will see these pages in more detail shortly.

Lines n.14 and n.15 contain the PHP variables that allow us to retrieve the data of the form fields: **$ _REQUEST ["field_name"]** ;. It is part of the so-called "*superglobals*" variables: that is, they are always available in every area of a PHP file.

Notice how **every PHP statement** must always end with a semicolon ";". If you don't put it, the server will return a **Parse error**:

When an error occurs, unless the PHP interpreter has the directive not to show them, the browser will display the type of error, the page where it occurred, and the line number in which it was detected. The first few times it may happen that you do not under-

<?php Building Real World PHP Applications ?>

stand the reason, but by reading the message carefully you will find the solution in a short time. The advice is to always check the presence of; at the end of instruction and to check not only the line mentioned by the error message but also the next line. With experience, you will immediately understand the reason that caused the error.

Once the value of the form field has been assigned to a variable, we can proceed to possibly modify its content or carry out checks based on our needs.

In the specific case, we see that the content of the form field retrieved from $ _REQUEST ["userk"] is assigned to the **$userk** variable; This variable is arbitrary, we can call it whatever we like: $username, $user, $foo, $a, etc. For convenience and to make the code more intelligible, I usually name the variables that retrieve the data of a form field with the name of the field itself. The form contained the field <input type="text" name="_userk_" size="20">, so I called the PHP variable _**$userk**_.

Line 16 checks the existence of the two variables, through the *isset()* function, which is equivalent to saying that the username and password fields of the form contain the text entered by the user and are *not empty*.

This verification takes place through a **control structure**. In our case, it is the control structure (or conditional statements) *if*. If executes the enclosing block of statements only if a certain condition is met. The statement block is enclosed in braces **{}**. In our example, the condition that must occur depends on the fact that the variables $userk and (through the logical operator **&&**) $pas-

<!=== Andrea Mauro Raimondi ===>

sk are not empty. To be true, the condition must verify that both variables exist. If the condition occurs, we carry out some checks on the variables (and in this case on the data received from the form). In the example code, lines 19 and 20 apply the **trim()** function, which is part of the functions that manipulate string (or textual) data. It does nothing but removes any whitespace, or, as we will see when dealing with data from an insert in the database, we may want to format the dates to make them compatible with the insertion in the database (which uses the format yyyy-mm-dd), or even add escape characters to avoid errors, as can happen with apostrophes. Php's functions enclose the variables, which are their arguments, in round brackets **()**. This happens for all functions written in PHP, see the following discussion. Once the spaces have been removed, in this example, we proceed to verify the existence of a user who has that username and password, by searching for the corrisponding record inside our database. I usually create a variable that contains the SQL to send to the database:

*$sqlb = "SELECT * *
FROM PHP_course_users
WHERE
username='$userk'
AND
password='$passk'
AND
active='1'";

In this case, we search in the database, in the table, for the record corresponding to the username and password sent by the form.

The typical structure to perform an SQL search is the following: the "**SELECT**" command is used, followed by the fields to be searched or by the generic "*****" which indicates all the fields, then the name of the table, and finally the condition: **SELECT * FROM table_name WHERE field1 = "x";** We will see in the appendix the most commonly used commands and selectors for SQL search.

You have to send that SQL command to the database now through PHP. This is the PHP code:

line 23: $resultb = **mysqli_query** ($connection, $sqlb) or die (mysqli_error ());

line 24: $ exists = **mysqli_num_rows** ($resultb);

The PHP *mysqli_query* function takes care of sending the SQL call, contained in the *$sqlb* variable to the database and returns the result of this call in the *$resultb* variable, which will then be manipulated to get the data from the query based on our needs. We note that mysqli_query has as its first argument the variable *$connection* which corresponds to the connection opened with database. In our application it is found in the file included, *zz_top_inc.php,* that we will see shortly.

Line 24 checks through the *mysqli_num_rows* function if the SQL query we sent just before returned non-empty lines. We put the result of this function in the variable *$exists.* Line 25 deals with verifying whether the value of *$exists* is or is not equal to or inferior to 0 (zero), that is, if the required data were not found. This is done through the *if* control. So this is the **if ($exists <= 0) {code block}** code. In our file, if there is no user with that username and password, the login form will be shown again, possibly reporting an error. If, on the other hand, the data correspond to a user in the

<!=== **Andrea Mauro Raimondi** ===>

database then we will create a session variable that will accompany the user and insert the data into the *logutenti_admin* table, which keeps track of active users, furthermore we will increase the counter of accesses related to that user, updating also the field with the date and time of the last access. We will display the link to continue within the back office, or we can directly redirect the user to a home page. Here is the result in case of success.

And the relative code. From lines 77 to 91 a random session variable is created, through some PHP functions that produce random numbers *rand()*. The number obtained is then passed to another *uniqid()* function that generates a unique ID based on the microtime (the current time in microseconds). In this way, we obtain a string that we will use for the user's session and will be inserted into the database.

In this block of code, we find two other SQL statements: INSERT and UPDATE. With the first, you insert the data in a table, with the second you update the data of one or more fields of a table.
The syntax for INSERT statement is:

INSERT INTO nome_tabella (campo1,campo2,[...]) values
('valore_campo1','valore_campo2',[...])

UPDATE statement:

UPDATE nome_tabella set
campo1='valore_campo1',campo2='valore_campo2',campox='valore_ca
mpox'

Each value assigned to a table field must be inserted between single quotes " ' ".
The SQL statements are assigned to a PHP variable and sent to the database with *mysqli_query()* function, the result of which is assigned to a variable that we will name as it suits us. I usually call it *$result*.
Let's see the files that are included in the *login.php* page, starting with *zz_top_inc.php*
The file contains the HTML code that defines the header used for all pages in the back office area

<!=== Andrea Mauro Raimondi ===>

```
1    <?php
2    //***************************************************
3    //AUTHOR: andrea raimondi info--AT--aredit.com
4    //file: header per tutte le pagine admin
5    //***************************************************
6    ?>
7    <!doctype html>
8    <html>
9    <head>
10   <title>...::: MY COMPANY - A Simple Product Catalog :::...</title>
11   <meta http-equiv="Content-type" content="text/html; charset=UTF-8">
12   <meta name="author" content="Andrea Raimondi - info--AT--aredit.com">
13   <meta name="editor" content="Andrea Raimondi">
14   <meta name="robots" content="noindex">
15   <link rel="shortcut icon" href="../img/favicon.ico" />
16   <link rel=StyleSheet href="../css/73160000.css" type="text/css" media=screen>
17   <style type="text/css">
18   a:link { color: #ff0000; }
19   a:active { color: #FFCC00; }
20   a:visited { color: #FF0000; }
21   </style></head>
22   <?php
23   include_once('connection_inc.php');
24   ?>
25   <body>
26   <center>
27   <table border=1 cellpadding=0 cellspacing=0 bgcolor="#ffffff">
28   <tr>
29   <td>
30
31   <table cellspacing=0 cellpadding=0 border=0 width="760" bgcolor="#9999cc">
32           <tr>
33           <td valign=top><img src="../img/php.gif" border=0 align=absmiddle></td>
34           <td valign=top align=center><h1>MYPHP COMPANY</h1></td>
35           <td valign=top align=right><img src="../img/php.gif" border=0 align=absmiddle></td>
36           </tr>
37   <tr bgcolor="#333366"><td colspan="3" height=10> </td></tr>
38   </table>
39
40   <table cellspacing=0 cellpadding=0 border=0 width="100%">
41   <tr>
42   <td valign=top align=center height=400>
43
44
```

This file contains the main table that forms the whole page, a sub-table with the logos and the name of our company, and another sub-table that contains the HTML and PHP code of the other pages. The *zz_bottom_inc.php* file will take care of closing the main table with the appropriate tags.

As we can see on line 23, in this file there is a file included: *connection_inc.php*. This file is responsible for establishing the connection to the database used by the application.

```php
1   <?php
2   //********************************************************
3   //AUTHOR: andrea raimondi info--AT--aredit.com
4   //file: file connessione
5   //********************************************************
6   ?>
7   <?php
8   $host='SERVER MYSQL';
9   $user='DB user';
10  $dbnome='DB name';
11  $pass='DB password';
12
13  $connection = mysqli connect("$host", "$user","$pass", "$dbnome");
14  |
15  if (mysqli connect errno()) {
16    echo "Failed to connect to MySQL: " . mysqli connect error();
17  }
18
19  ?>
```

This connection type, valid for a MySQL database, can be used in any application, changing the name of the database and its login data. I prefer to insert it in a separate file and then include it in the header of other files: I will no longer have to worry about managing the connection. Unless, of course, you need files with a different header. In this case we have to include the connection file directly in the files that need to interact with the database.

<!=== Andrea Mauro Raimondi ===>

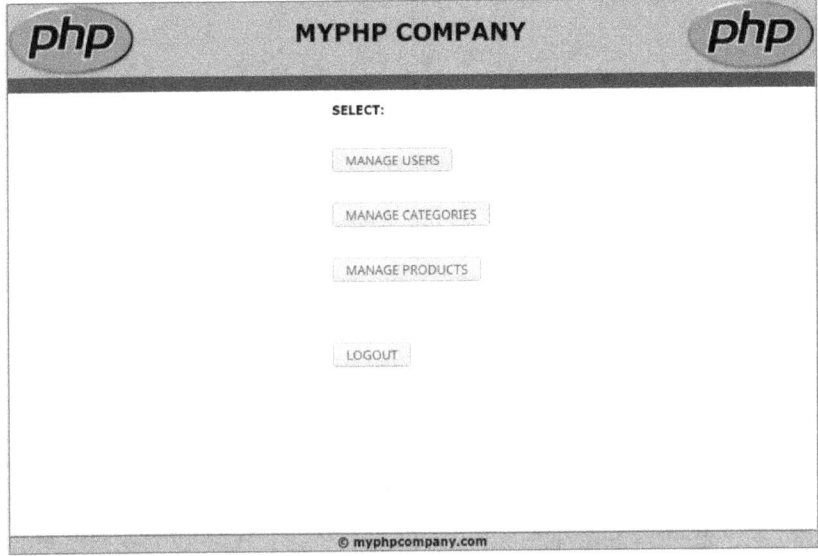

Once logged in, we will access the *menu.php* page

This in the code:

```php
<?php
//*********************************************
//AUTHOR: andrea raimondi info: AI  aredit.com
//file: menu
//*********************************************
?>
<?php
include('zz top inc.php');
?>
<?php
include('utility inc.php');
?>
<P>
<table border=0 cellpadding=0 cellspacing=0>
<tr><td>SELECT:</td></tr>
<tr><td><br/><br/></td></tr>
<?php
if ($xlevel=="0") {
?>
<tr><td><input type="button" onclick="document.location.href='users.php?mysessionid=<?php print $mysessionid;?>&idu=<?php print $idu;?>';" value="MANAGE USERS"></td></tr>
<tr><td><br/><br/></td></tr>
}
?>
<tr><td><input type="button" onclick="document.location.href='categories.php?mysessionid=<?php print $mysessionid;?>&idu=<?php print $idu;?>';" value="MANAGE CATEGORIES"></td></tr>
<tr><td><br/><br/></td></tr>
<tr><td><input type="button" onclick="document.location.href='products.php?mysessionid=<?php print $mysessionid;?>&idu=<?php print $idu;?>';" value="MANAGE PRODUCTS"></td></tr>
```

and

<?php Building Real World PHP Applications ?>

```
13   <tr><td>SELECT:</td></tr>
16   <tr><td><br/><br/></td></tr>
17   <?php
18   if ($xlevel=="0") {
19   ?>
20   <tr><td><input type="button" onclick="document.location.href='users.php?mysessionid=<?php print $mysessionid;?>&idu=<?php print $idu;?
     >';" value="MANAGE USERS"></td></tr>
21   <tr><td><br/><br/></td></tr>
22   <?php
23   }
24   ?>
25   <tr><td><input type="button" onclick="document.location.href='categories.php?mysessionid=<?php print $mysessionid;?>&idu=<?php print
     $idu;?>';" value="MANAGE CATEGORIES"></td></tr>
26   <tr><td><br/><br/></td></tr>
27   <tr><td><input type="button" onclick="document.location.href='products.php?mysessionid=<?php print $mysessionid;?>&idu=<?php print
     $idu;?>';" value="MANAGE PRODUCTS"></td></tr>
28
29   <tr><td><br/><br/></td></tr>
30   <tr><td><br/><br/></td></tr>
31
32   <tr><td><input type="button" onclick="document.location.href='logout.php?mysessionid=<?php print $mysessionid;?>&idu=<?php print $idu;?
     >';" value="LOGOUT"></td></tr>
33   </table>
34
35   </P>
36
37   <?php
38   include('zz_bottom_inc.php');
39   ?>
40
```

This page displays four buttons for links to different management pages. A button takes you to the page where we will manage the users who can access the system. Another leads to the page with which we will manage the product categories. The products themselves will be managed by a special page accessible with the third button. Finally, we find the button to log out and deactivate the current session.

Studying the code of this page, we note that it includes a new PHP file "utility_inc.php" and that the execution of a block of code depends on the occurrence of a condition: that is if the variable $xlevel$ is equal to 0 or no. By convention, we have decided that the system administrator, the super admin, is identified by an access level of 0 (zero). Any other possible levels will therefore have a level with a number greater than zero. These levels can be users in consultation only of the data, or users who can only manage the insertion and/or modification of products. In short, it depends on how we have to structure the access levels for a given application.

<!=== Andrea Mauro Raimondi ===>

In our case, the data will be saved in the *"level"* column of the *PHP_course_users* table. Somewhere we will have to insert some PHP code that will have to retrieve the data relating to the user level and, based on it, show or not certain areas or functionalities of the application.

In our case, this code is found in the aforementioned *utility_inc.php* file. Through this page, we will also carry out checks on the validity of the user session.

```php
1    <?php
2    $idu = $_REQUEST["idu"];
3    $mysessionid = $_REQUEST["mysessionid"];
4    $strquery = "idu=$idu&mysessionid=$mysessionid";
5    if ($mysessionid == "") {
6        $idu = 0;
7    }
8    else {
9        $sql = "select * from PHP_course_logutenti_admin
10               WHERE SESSIONID='$mysessionid' AND STATE='1'";
11       $resultbl = mysqli_query($connection,$sql) or die(mysqli_error());
12       $esistel=mysqli_num_rows($resultbl);
13       if ($esistel > 0) {
14           $sqlb = "SELECT * FROM PHP_course_users WHERE iduser=$idu AND active='1'";
15           $resultb = mysqli_query($connection,$sqlb) or die(mysqli_error());
16           $ValoriRigabl = mysqli_fetch_array($resultb);
17           $xlevel = $ValoriRigabl["level"];
18           $xname = $ValoriRigabl["name"];
19       }
20       else {
21           $idu = 0;
22       }
23   }
24   if ($idu == 0) {
25       include_once('zz_top_inc.php');
26       print "<font color=\"#cc0000\" size=\"+3\">SESSION EXPIRED!</font><br>";
27       print "You need to <a href=\"login.php\">login</a>";
28       include('zz_bottom_inc.php');
29       exit;
30   }
31   ?>
```

Lines 2 and 3 through $ _REQUEST[] retrieve the values of the *idu* and *myssessionid* variables, passed by the calling page through the link, in this case, *login.php,* and assign them to the PHP variables *$idu* and *$mysessionid*. In this case, I always prefer to name the data that is passed from one page to another in the same way.

With line 4 I create a variable that comes in handy when we have to build the query string to match the various links and that allows us to pass the session parameters. So, in this case, we create two session variables that are checked when each page is loaded: *$idu* which is the reference to the user ID, and *$mysessionid* which is the reference to the random variable created at the beginning of the session through login.

The page now performs the necessary checks on these variables: first, check that *$mysessionid* is not empty. If it is, the variable *$idu* is set equal to 0. If, on the other hand, *$mysessionid* is not empty, check the *PHP_course_logutenti_admin* table to see if its value belongs to an active session. The relative SELECT looks for whether the value exists in the SESSIONID field and whether the state is active, ie that the STATE field is equal to "1". We will see in analyzing the logout procedure that the STATE field will be set equal to zero when the user, by logging out, ends his work session.

If the data is found and there is therefore an active session, the system searches for information relating to the user utilizing his ID, which is a unique identifier, automatically generated from the MySQL table. This is because we have created this field (*iduser*) with the *auto_increment* attribute.

For convenience, I report the SQL code that creates the *iduser* field and the table *PHP_course_users*:

```
CREATE TABLE `PHP_course_users` (
  `iduser` int(4) NOT NULL auto_increment,
  `name` varchar(250) NOT NULL default '',
  `username` varchar(50) NOT NULL default '',
  `password` varchar(50) NOT NULL default '',
  `active` int(2) NOT NULL default '0',
  `level` int(2) NOT NULL default '1',
  `lastaccess` datetime NOT NULL default '0000-00-00 00:00:00',
  `naccess` int(4) NOT NULL default '0',
  PRIMARY KEY (`iduser`)
) TYPE=MyISAM
```

After the database search, we create the $xlevel and $xname variables that we will also use in other files, lines 9 to 20.

If, on the other hand, there is no active session or the same value is not found among the records of the SESSIONID field, the code will set the *$idu* variable to 0 (zero), as shown in line 22.

At this point, the system evaluates the proper content of the $ idu variable. If it is equal to 0 (zero), then as we have just seen, the session is invalid, an error message is displayed.

In case of an error, we have to try the login again.

If the menu appears, we will choose the item we need.

Let's start by managing the categories of the products we want to show. By clicking on the MANAGE CATEGORIES button, the list of categories already present in the database is displayed, specifically in the *PHP_course_categories* table.

<!=== **Andrea Mauro Raimondi** ===>

CATEGORIES MANAGEMENT

Let's take the category management of our application as an example of managing a MySQL table. The logical structure with which the file is built will serve as a basis for all cases in which operations are performed on a table. Indeed, for most interactions in a back office area.

I recommend studying it and understanding it well. We will only have to change the names of the variables, the fields of the table we are working on, and the names of the form fields. It will become a semi-automatic job. You must first understand precisely the functioning of the PHP page, its structure.

As we see on the following page, the file is composed of a *switch()* type control on the *$action* variable and two functions, *formcategory()*, which creates the form for interacting with the user and *list_record()* which displays a table with the data already present in the database, and the commands to modify or delete them.

Functions in PHP, and all programming languages, are nothing more than blocks of code that can receive input data, the arguments of the function, perform operations, processing the input data, and return the result. In our *categories.php* file, the *list_record()* function has no input data because it takes care of retrieving the data present in the database, with a query, and send them to the browser in the form of an HTML table. We will see in detail in next pages.

```php
1    <?php
2    //*********************************************
3    //AUTHOR: andrea raimondi info--AT--aredit.com
4    //file: manage categories
5    //*********************************************
6    ?>
7    <?php
8    include('zz_top_inc.php');
9    include('utility_inc.php');
10
11   $action = $_REQUEST["action"];
12   $idcategory = $_REQUEST["idcategory"];
13   $category = $_REQUEST["category"];
14 ▶ switch ($action) {
88   }
89   ?>
90   <?php
91   ###############################################
92   ###############form category###################
93   ###############################################
94 ▶ function formcategory() {
117  }
118  ###############################################
119  ##############function list categories#########
120  ###############################################
121 ▶ function list_record() {
182  }
183  ?>|
184  <?php
185  //footer;
186  include('zz_bottom_inc.php');
```

The *switch($action)* control structure of line 14 performs checks on the value of the *$action* variable. This variable comes from the form.

The *switch()* has the following cases:

__case "modify"__: takes care of finding the data relating to a particular record within the *PHP_course_categories* table and then sending to the form that will display them to eventually modify.

__case "delete"__: takes care of deleting a record from the table, it is possible to perform checks before the actual deletion of the record

__case "add"__: takes care of enhancing some variables and sending them to the form for creating a new record. In this case, we set the *$idcategory* variable to 0 (zero), which will tell the system that it is a new record when the data is sent to the server from the form.

__case "save"__: takes care of saving the data of a record. As we will see, based on the value of the *$idcategory* variable, the system will send a query of type *INSERT*, to create a new record, or of type *UPDATE*, to modify the data of an existing record. The discriminating value lies in the fact that *$idcategory* is greater than zero, which indicates that the record is to be modified, or equal to zero, that is, that the record is new.

__case default:__ it is the code executed if none of the previous conditions occur. In our file, this happens when the file does not receive the *$action* variable or when it is *empty*: therefore when you call from another page or from the Start menu, or when you want to view the list of records of this table.

Clearly, the names of "case"(s) are arbitrary but it is always better they are indicative of what they contain, the same goes for the names of variables and functions.

The *switch* structure will be the same for the various table management files, as in the case of *user* or *product* management. The same would be true if we had other tables to manage and interact with.

Now let's see the code in detail starting from calling the *categories.php* page from the initial menu. Let's follow the path of the data and his logic. As we have seen, a check is performed on the value of the *$action* variable. If we arrive from the menu page, this value does not exist, so the *switch* will execute the code contained in its *default* section. This will only call the code contained in the *list_record()* function. Always remember to put *break* at the end of each switch statement, otherwise, the PHP parser will execute the following *switch* statement, as we will see in the *case save*. The *list_record()* function has the purpose to creating an HTML table with the data retrieved from the *categories* table of the database. Here is the complete code of the *list_record()* function.

<!=== Andrea Mauro Raimondi ===>

```php
121    ###########################################################
122  function list_record() {
123    $strmsg = "PRODUCTS CATEGORIES LIST";
124    global $idu, $mysessionid, $strquery,$connection;
125    ?>
126    <script language="javascript">
127    function del(url) {
128      if (confirm("DATA WILL BE DELETED!\nDo you want to continue?")){
129        document.location.href=url;
130      }
131    }
132    </script>
133    <br>
134    <table width="100%">
135    <tr>
136    <td colspan=8 align=center class="ss"><?php print $strmsg; ?></td>
137    </tr>
138    <tr>
139    <td align=center><a href="menu.php?<?php print $strquery; ?>">[ MENU ]</a>
140    <a href="<?php print $_SERVER['PHP_SELF'];?>?<?php print $strquery; ?>&action=add">[ NEW RECORD ]</a></td>
141    </tr>
142    </table>
143    <table width="100%" cellspacing=2 cellpadding=0 border=0>
144    <tr>
145    <td colspan=8 align=right>
146    </td>
147    </tr>
148    <tr class="titolocampo">
149    <td>Category</td>
150    <td> </td>
151    </tr>
152    <?php
153    $bgc1="#cccccc";
154    $bgc2="#dddddd";
155    $bgc = $bgc1;
156    if ($bgc == $bgc1) {
157      $bgc = $bgc2;
158    }
159    else {
160      $bgc=$bgc1;
161    }
162    $query = "select * from PHP_course_categories ORDER BY category";
163    $result = mysqli_query($connection,$query) or die(mysqli_error());
164    while ($ValoriRiga = mysqli_fetch_array($result)) {
165      $idcategory = $ValoriRiga["idcategory"];
166      $category = $ValoriRiga["category"];
167    ?>
168    <tr bgcolor="<?php print $bgc; ?>">
169    <td><?php print $category; ?></td>
170    <td align=center>
171    <?php
172    print "<a href=\"categories.php?$strquery&idcategory=$idcategory&action=modify\">[ Modify ]</a>
173    <a href=\"#\" onclick=\"del('categories.php?$strquery&idcategory=$idcategory&action=delete');\">[ Delete ]</a>
174    ";
175    ?>
176    </td>
177    </tr>
178    <?php
179    }
180    ?>
```

Like any function, the *list_record()* code is enclosed in braces {...}. It does not need arguments because some variables are defined as global and therefore can be used inside the function, in more precise terms the *scope* of a variable marked as **global** concerns all the code in use and not just one of its portion, how can it be a function. Variables created within a function have a **local** scope: their value can only be seen within the function itself. Line 124, therefore, defines as global *$idu, $mysessionid, $strquery, $connection*; Basically, they are the *session variables* that we use

```
147    </tr>
148    <tr class="titolocampo">
149 |  <td>Category</td>
150    <td> </td>
151    </tr>
152    <?php
153    $bgc1="#cccccc";
154    $bgc2="#dddddd";
155    $bgc = $bgc1;
156 ▼ if ($bgc == $bgc1) {
157    $bgc = $bgc2;
158    }
159 ▼ else {
160    $bgc=$bgc1;
161    }
162    $query = "select * from PHP_course_categories ORDER BY category";
163    $result = mysqli_query($connection,$query) or die(mysqli_error());
164 ▼ while ($ValoriRiga = mysqli_fetch_array($result)) {
165    $idcategory = $ValoriRiga["idcategory"];
166    $category = $ValoriRiga["category"];
167    ?>
168    <tr bgcolor="<?php print $bgc; ?>">
169    <td><?php print $category; ?></td>
170 |  <td align=center><?php print "<a href=\"$_SERVER['PHP_SELF']?$strquery&idcategory=$idcategory&action=modify\">[
  - |  Modifica ]</a><a href=\"#\" onclick=\"del('categories.php?$strquery&idcategory=$idcategory&action=delete');\">[
  - |  Cancella ]</a>"?></td>
171    </tr>
172    <?php
173    }
174    ?>
175    </table>
176    <?php
177    }
178    ?>
```

throughout the back office area (*$idu, $mysessionid, $strquery*), and the connection variable, *$connection*. On line 123 we define a *string type* variable *$strmsg*="PRODUCTS CATEGORIES LIST"; which will be used as the title for the HTML table in line 136. I prefer to use a variable external to the table because it allows me to reuse it in the other pages, which are mostly copies of

<!=== **Andrea Mauro Raimondi** ===>

this one, taken as a model. Furthermore, if needed, I can add more text to the variable, passed by any other variable and concatenate it with *$strmsg: $strmsg=*"*$another_var $strmsg*";

Lines 126-131 define a block of javascript code that creates a function activated when a record's *delete button* is clicked. The javascript function will activate a warning, an **alert**, asking the user if he is sure he wants to delete the record. This javascript function could also be inserted after the HTML table.

Then there are two tables, the first, at lines 134-142, creates a line with the links to return to the menu and to add a new record, while the second will display the HTML table containing the data taken from the database.

Returning to the first table and the links it displays, this is the link that is used <?php print $_SERVER['PHP_SELF'];?>?<?php print $strquery; ?>&action=add;

As we can see, we pass the *session variables* through the *$strquery* variable (which if you remember is defined in the *utility_inc.php* file) and the **action** for the next page (in this case it is the same page, *categories.php*), through the $*action* variable of the query string. This variable is the same that will be treated by the **switch** seen above, precisely in the *case add*: code block, lines 48-52.

```
46    ############## add record ##############################################
47    ########################################################################
48    case "add":
49        $idcategory = "0";
50        $msg = "NEW CATEGORY";
51        formcategory();
52        break;
53    ########################################################################
54    ############## save record #############################################
55    ########################################################################
56    case "save":
57        if ($idcategory=="0") { //new category;
58            $sql = "insert into PHP_course_categories (category) values ('$category')";
59            $result = mysqli_query($connection,$sql);
60            if (! $result)
61            {
62                echo "<b>Record was not inserted!</b>";
63            }
64            else
65            {
66                echo "Record added.";
67            }
68        }
69        else { //update record;
70            $sql = "update PHP_course_categories set category='$category' where idcategory=$idcategory";
71            $result = mysqli_query($connection,$sql);
72            if (! $result)
73            {
74                echo "<b>Record not updated!</b>";
75            }
76            else
77            {
78                echo "Record modified.";
79            }
80        }
81        //break; // <======== Note the commented line to make sure to perform the default switch code
82    ########################################################################
83    ############## default: list ###########################################
84    ########################################################################
85    default:
86        list();
87        break;
```

<!=== Andrea Mauro Raimondi ===>

In the second html table present in the *list_record()* function we can see how the records from a MySQL table are retrieved and displayed by php. In the code of lines 162-173 we find:

$query = "select * from PHP_course_categories ORDER BY category";
$result=mysqli_query($connection, $query) or die (mysqli_error());

The variable that contains the SQL command *$query* is created then used to send the query to the database through the PHP *mysql_query* function, already seen previously.

The data returned from the database is then looped through the PHP while command. The data is assigned to the *$ValoriRiga* variable which is a variable of type array, through the PHP function mysqli_fetch_array, which has as argument the result of the previously sent query.

$V*aloriRiga*=mysqli_fetch_array($result);

The loop on that *array* allows us to define a variable for each field returned by the query and to insert it within a cell of the HTML table. Here is the code of the while loop:

```
$query = "select * from PHP_course_categories ORDER BY category";
$result = mysqli_query($connection,$query) or die(mysqli_error());
while ($ValoriRiga = mysqli_fetch_array($result)) {
$idcategory = $ValoriRiga["idcategory"];
$category = $ValoriRiga["category"];
?>
<tr bgcolor="<?php print $bgc; ?>">
<td><?php print $category; ?></td>
<td align=center>
<?php
print "
173   <a href=\"categories.php?$strquery&idcategory=$idcategory&action=modify\">[ Modify ]</a>
<a href=\"#\" onclick=\"del('categories.php?$strquery&idcategory=$idcategory&action=delete');\">[ Delete ]</a>
";
?>
</td>
</tr>
<?php
}
```

For each record, a row of the table is created, using <tr> </tr>, and the category *name* and *links* to edit the text and to delete the record are displayed.

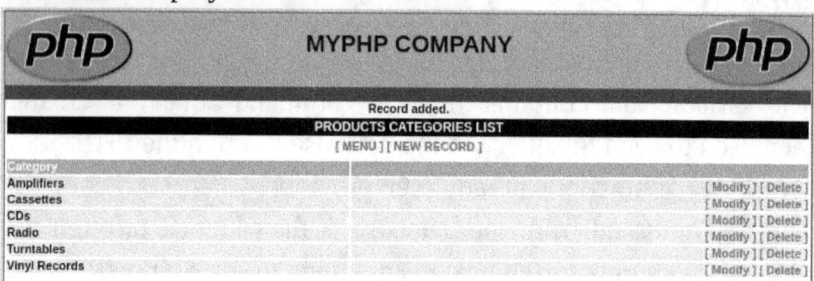

As you can see the links have respectively
*action=**modify*** and *action=**delete***: once clicked, they will lead to execute the corresponding code block within the switch.

```
16    ############# modify record ####################################
17    ##############################################################
18    case "modify":
19        $query = "select * from PHP_course_categories where idcategory=$idcategory";
20        $result = mysqli_query($connection,$query) or die(mysqli_error());
21  ▼     while ($ValoriRiga = mysqli_fetch_array($result)) {
22        $idcategory = $ValoriRiga["idcategory"];
23        $category = $ValoriRiga["category"];
24        }
25        $msg = "MODIFY CATEGORY $category";
26        formcategory();
27        break;
28    ##############################################################
29    ############# delete record ##################################
30    ##############################################################
31    case "delete":
32        //N.B. verificare se esistono prodotti nella category.
33        $sql  = "delete from PHP_course_categories where idcategory=$idcategory";
34        $result = mysqli_query($connection,$sql);
35  ▼       if (! $result)
36            {
37  |         echo "<b>The record was not deleted!</b>";
38            }
39        else
40  ▼       {
41            echo "Record deleted.";
42            }
43  |       list_record();
44        break;
```

<!=== **Andrea Mauro Raimondi** ===>

If the back-office user wants to delete a record, he will click on the "*Delete*" link in the row corresponding to the record to be deleted, the relative code is found in line 174. At this point the javascript function is activated which takes care of displaying a message *alert*:

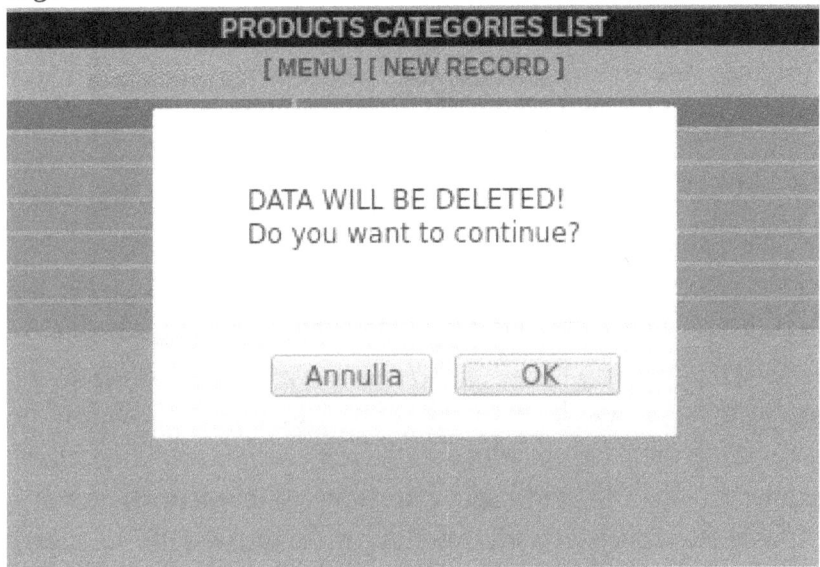

If the user intends to continue, by clicking on the "**OK**" button, the page will continue to the URL indicated in the javascript function. If the user does not want to continue deleting the record, by clicking on "**Cancel**", the page will stay with the current display, that is, the list of records.

function del(url) {
  if (confirm("DATA WILL BE DELETED!\nDo you want to continue?")){
    document.location.href=url;
  }

<?php Building Real World PHP Applications ?>

```
126  <script language="javascript">
127  function del(url) {
128      if (confirm("DATA WILL BE DELETED!\nDo you want to continue?")){
129      document.location.href=url;
130      }
131  }
132  </script>
```

As you can see from the javascript code, the code block must be inserted between the <script> and </script> tags, this will make the server and the browser understand to treat the content as javascript in this case.

You create the *function*, which has the same construction as PHP, by enclosing it in braces **{}**. In this case, we want javascript to create a confirm object, a confirmation window, displaying the text that is between the double-quotes. In case of confirmation by the user, when he clicks the "*OK*" button, the code between the confirm braces will be executed. In our case, the browser will be directed to the page contained in the **url** variable passed as an argument of the function itself, which we called **del(url)**. As previously mentioned, this url is nothing more than the call to the categories.php page, passing in addition to the session variables also the $action variable with *value=delete*.

So let's see how the code called by this user action, the switch code block, behaves with the case "*delete*".

Below is the complete PHP code: the purpose is to delete the record from the table by means of the unique reference given by the idcategory variable passed by the previous querystring. If you remember, in the *PHP_course_categories* table, *idcategory* is a *unique field* (each record has a different value than that field) of

<!=== Andrea Mauro Raimondi ===>

type *auto_increment*. We write the SQL code for deleting a record, inserting it in a PHP variable, *$sql*, line 33. We execute the query with the usual PHP *mysqli_query* function, line 34. Then we evaluate the result of the query using the value returned by the server and stored in the *$result* variable. The function returns *false* on failure. For this reason, the check that we perform through the *if* statement, verifies this condition, line 35. The operator "!", Means *not*, is a logical PHP operator. In our case, the expression literally means: "if $result is not true, then executes the following block of code". The SQL call for delete a record uses the DELETE command, which has the following syntax: *DELETE from table_name WHERE condition to check*.

```
31    case "delete":
32        //N.B. Do we have some products in this category?
33        $sql  = "delete from PHP_course_categories where idcategory=$idcategory";
34        $result = mysqli_query($connection,$sql);
35            if (! $result)
36            {
37            echo "<b>The record was not deleted!</b>";
38            }
39            else
40            {
41            echo "Record deleted.";
42            }
43            list_record();
44        break;
```

If the user wishes to *modify* a record, he will click on "*Modify*" link:

```
173     <a href=\"categories.php?$strquery&idcategory=$idcategory&action=modify\">[ Modify ]</a>
```

as we can see, in addition to the session variables, contained in *$strquery* variable, defined in the file *included utility_inc.php*, the *idcategory* variable will also be sent, which will have as its value the unique ID of the table relating to the record to be modified,

and *action*, this time with the value *"modify"*. This link leads to
the execution of the *switch case "modify"*: code block

```
18    case "modify":
19        $query = "select * from PHP_course_categories where idcategory=$idcategory";
20        $result = mysqli_query($connection,$query) or die(mysqli_error());
21  ▾     while ($ValoriRiga = mysqli_fetch_array($result)) {
22            $idcategory = $ValoriRiga["idcategory"];
23            $category = $ValoriRiga["category"];
24        }
25        $msg = "MODIFY CATEGORY $category";
26        formcategory();
27        break;
```

The purpose is simply to retrieve the values of the record with the
desired *idcategory* and pass the data to the function that creates
the HTML form. Once displayed within the fields of the html
form, the user can modify the data and save them in the database
table. To do this we create a variable that contains the SQL command, a SELECT; we execute the query in the database and through the *mysqli_fetch_array* function, we retrieve the data and
assign them to appropriate PHP variables that will be displayed in
the HTML form. This is displayed by the function
formcategory(). This function, as we will see, using the aforementioned variables *global* and therefore can access them even if
created outside the function itself. We also create the *$msg* varia-
ble, which will contain the text to be displayed as the title of the
HTML form.

MODIFY CATEGORY Radio	
Category	Radio
	Save

<!=== Andrea Mauro Raimondi ===>

This is the final result before the modification of the text relating to the "Radio" category. Below, here is the code that generates this form.

```php
function formcategory() {
  global $idu, $mysessionid, $strquery, $msg;
  global $idcategory, $category;
  ?>
  <table width=400 border=0 cellpadding=0 cellspacing=3 bgcolor="#cccccc">
    <form action="<?php print $_SERVER['PHP_SELF']; ?>" method="post" name="form1">
    <input type="hidden" name="action" value="save">
    <input type="hidden" name="idcategory" value="<?php print $idcategory; ?>">
    <input type="hidden" name="idu" value="<?php print $idu; ?>">
    <input type="hidden" name="mysessionid" value="<?php print $mysessionid; ?>">
    <tr>
      <td colspan=2 class="ss" align=center><?php print $msg; ?></td>
    </tr>
    <tr>
      <td align=right >Category</td>
      <td align=left valign=top><input type="text" size="40" maxlength="100" name="category"
        value="<?php print $category; ?>"></td>
    </tr>
    <tr>
      <td colspan=2 align=center><input type="submit" name="invia" value="Save"></td>
    </tr>
    </form>
  </table>
  <?php
}
```

As you can see, the *formcategory()* function has the purpose of displaying an HTML table that formats a form, in this case consisting of only a field, the *name* of the category. The form field is an <input type = "text"> which will have as its value the name of the *category* retrieved from the variable whose content was found in the database by the previous *switch* operation with *case "modify"*. It is useful to name the fields of the form, through the *name attribute*, in the same way as we have called the *fields of the table*: in this way we know precisely what data we are working on and what they must do within the page and in the application. Lines 100-103 create some *hidden* type fields, these will not be seen by the user in the form, but allow you to send "*service*" data, such as, for example, session variables or other data useful for other operations. In our case, we send in this way both the *action* variable, which has *value=save*. This will allow the PHP page to execute the "*save*" case code block in our *switch*.

<!=== Andrea Mauro Raimondi ===>

Once you have changed the category name and clicked on the "*Save*" button, the data will be sent again to the *categories.php* file, which this time will execute the code block you find below:

```
55    ###############################################################
56    case "save":
57        if ($idcategory=="0") { //new category
58            $sql = "insert into PHP_course_categories (category) values ('$category')";
59            $result = mysqli_query($connection,$sql);
60            if (! $result)
61            {
62            echo "<b>Record was not inserted!</b>";
63            }
64            else
65            {
66            echo "Record added.";
67            }
68        }
69        else { //update record
70            $sql = "update PHP_course_categories set category='$category' where idcategory=$idcategory";
71            $result = mysqli_query($connection,$sql);
72            if (! $result)
73            {
74            echo "<b>Record not updated!</b>";
75            }
76            else
77            {
78            echo "Record modified.";
79            }
80        }
81        //break; // <======= Note the commented line to make sure to perform the default switch code
```

This block of code is divided into two sections, based on the value of the *$idcategory* variable. If this is equal to zero, if (*$idcategory* == "0"), the data will be added to the table because we are in the case of a new record; otherwise, the data relating to the record with idcategory equal to the value of the $idcategory variable, is changed. In the first case the SQL statement will be of type *INSERT*, in the second of type *UPDATE*, respectively lines 58 and 70. A note on line 81, in which the *break* switch command has been commented, and therefore disabled. In this way, the execution of the *switch* instructions does *not stop* and the following instruction in the list of cases is executed: that is, the default instruction that calls the *list_record()* function is executed. If no errors occurred we will see the renamed category. Here is the list with the category changed from "Radio" to "Vintage Radio":

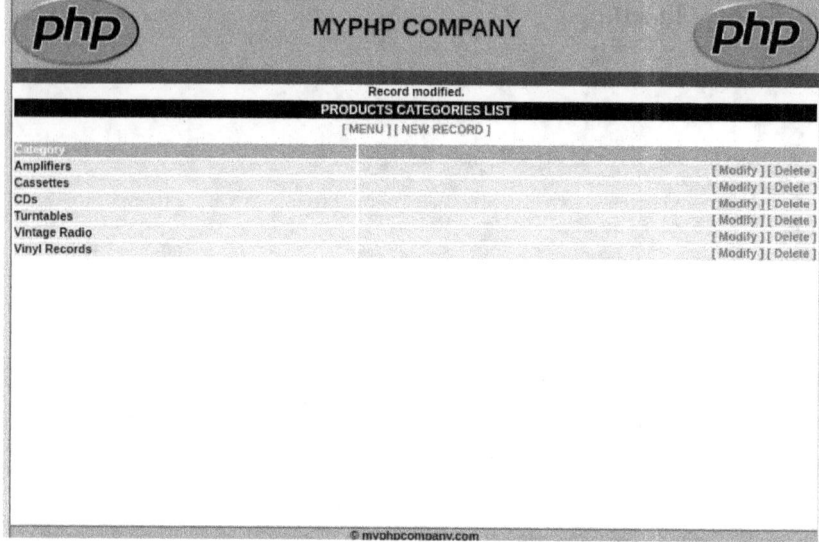

After having created the appropriate categories for our products, we return to the main menu and select the button for *product management,* which we see in the next chapter.

<!=== Andrea Mauro Raimondi ===>

GESTIONE PRODOTTI

For convenience, this is the structure of the table that we will manage:

```
CREATE TABLE `PHP_course_products` (
  `idproduct` int(4) NOT NULL auto_increment,
  `idcategory` int(4) NOT NULL default '0',
  `product_name` varchar(255) NOT NULL default '',
  `description` text NOT NULL,
  `quantity` int(4) NOT NULL default '0',
  `price` decimal(10,2) NOT NULL default '0.00',
  `tax` int(2) NOT NULL default '0',
  `img` varchar(250) NOT NULL default '',
  PRIMARY KEY (`idproduct`)
)
```

As we can see, we have to manage more fields in the table, so we will have a form with more fields, including the *idcategory* field that comes from the *PHP_course_categories* table. In this case, that field defines in a one-to-many relationship between the two tables: a field from the *PHP_course_categories* table can be found many times in the *PHP_course_products* table. We find table fields of different types, such as *text, decimal, int, varchar*.

Conceptually, the management of this table is the same as seen for the category table. The structure of the .php file is similar, the *names* of the variables and *related fields* will change. So you can simply copy the text of the *categories.php* file into a new one that

<?php Building Real World PHP Applications ?>

we call *products.php* and change the names of the fields and variables as said.

We will get this structure:

```
4    //file: products
5    //***********************************************
6    ?>
7    <?php
8    include('zz_top_inc.php');
9    include('utility_inc.php');
10   //recupero valori form
11   $action = $_REQUEST["action"];
12   $idproduct = $_REQUEST["idproduct"];
13   $idcategory = $_REQUEST["idcategory"];
14   $product_name = $_REQUEST["product_name"];
15   $description = $_REQUEST["description"];
16   $quantity = $_REQUEST["quantity"];
17   $price = $_REQUEST["price"];
18   $tax = $_REQUEST["tax"];
19   $img = $_REQUEST["img"];
20
21   switch ($action) {
132  }
133  ?>
134  <?php
135  ###############################################
136  ##############form products###############
137  ###############################################
138  function formproduct() {
209  }
210  ###############################################
211  ############## function list records  #######
212  ###############################################
213  function list_records() {
289  }
290  ?>
291  <?php
292  //footer della pagina;
293  include('zz_bottom_inc.php');
294  ?>
```

Very similar to the one already seen.

<!=== **Andrea Mauro Raimondi** ===>

Let's go into the details of the particularities of product management. Once you have clicked on the "MANAGE PRODUCTS" menu button,

you reach "*products.php*" page which displays the list of products in the database:

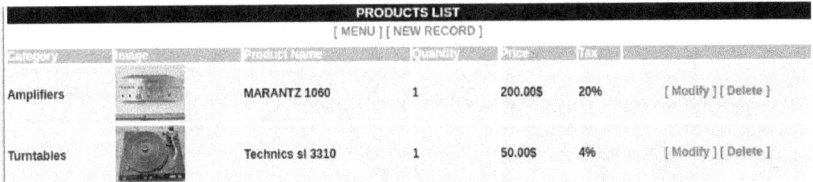

Category	Image	Product Name	Quantity	Price	Tax	
Amplifiers		MARANTZ 1060	1	200.00$	20%	[Modify] [Delete]
Turntables		Technics sl 3310	1	50.00$	4%	[Modify] [Delete]

This screen is the result of calling the *list_records()* function, which contains the HTML table populated with the records taken from the product table. You can see it on the following pages:

```php
210  function list_records() {
211    $strmsg = "PRODUCTS LIST";
212    global $idu, $mysessionid, $strquery,$connection;
213
214    ?>
215  <script language="javascript">
216  function del(url) {
217      if (confirm("DATA WILL BE DELETED!\nDo you want to continue?")){
218      document.location.href=url;
219      }
220  }
221  </script>
222  <br>
223  <table width="100%">
224  <tr>
225  <td colspan=8 align=center class="ss"><?php print $strmsg; ?></td>
226  </tr>
227  <tr>
228  <td align=center><a href="menu.php?<?php print $strquery; ?>">[ MENU ]</a>
229  <a href="<?php print $PHP_SELF;?>?<?php print $strquery; ?>&action=add">[ NEW RECORD ]</a></td>
230  </tr>
231  </table>
232  <table width="100%" cellspacing=2 cellpadding=0 border=0>
233
234  <tr>
235  <td colspan=8 align=right>
236  </td>
237  </tr>
238  <tr class="titolocampo">
239  <td>Category</td>
240  <td>Image</td>
241  <td nowrap>Product Name</td>
242  <td>Quantity</td>
243  <td>Price</td>
244  <td>Tax</td>
245  <td> </td>
246  </tr>
247  <?php
248  $bgc1="#cccccc";
249  $bgc2="#dddddd";
250  $bgc = $bgc1;
251
252  if ($bgc == $bgc1) {
253  $bgc = $bgc2;
254  }
255  else {
256  $bgc=$bgc1;
257  }
258  $query = "select * from PHP_course_products ORDER BY product_name";
259  $result = mysqli_query($connection,$query) or die(mysqli_error());
260  while ($ValoriRiga = mysqli_fetch_array($result)) {
261      $idproduct = $ValoriRiga["idproduct"];
262      $idcategory = $ValoriRiga["idcategory"];
263      $product_name = $ValoriRiga["product_name"];
264      $description = $ValoriRiga["description"];
265      $quantity = $ValoriRiga["quantity"];
266      $price = $ValoriRiga["price"];
267      $tax = $ValoriRiga["tax"];
268      $img = $ValoriRiga["img"];
269
270      //find category name
271      $sql = "select * from PHP_course_categories where idcategory='$idcategory'";
272      $result2 = mysqli_query($connection,$sql) or die(mysqli_error());
273      $ValoriRiga2 = mysqli_fetch_array($result2);
274      $category_name = $ValoriRiga2["category"];
```

<!=== Andrea Mauro Raimondi ===>

```
765        $quantity = $ValoriRiga["quantity"];
266        $price = $ValoriRiga["price"];
267        $tax = $ValoriRiga["tax"];
268        $img = $ValoriRiga["img"];
269
270        //find category name
271        $sql = "select * from PHP course_categories where idcategory='$idcategory'";
272        $result2 = mysqli_query($connection,$sql) or die(mysqli_error());
273        $ValoriRiga2 = mysqli_fetch_array($result2);
274        $category_name = $ValoriRiga2["category"];
275    ?>
276    <tr bgcolor="<?php print $bgc; ?>">
277    <td><?php print $category_name; ?></td>
278    <td><img src="../img/<?php print $img; ?>" height="50"></td>
279    <td nowrap><?php print $product_name; ?></td>
280    <td><?php print $quantity; ?></td>
281    <td><?php print $price; ?>$</td>
282    <td><?php print $tax; ?>%</td>
283    <td align=center><?php print "<a href=\"products.php?$strquery&idproduct=$idproduct&action=modify\">[ Modify ]</
  -    a> <a href=\"#\" onclick=\"del('prodotti.php?$strquery&idproduct=$idproduct&action=delete');\">[ Delete ]</a>"?
       ></td>
284    </tr>
285    <?php
286        }
287    ?>
288    </table>
289    <?php
290        }
291    ?>
```

As you can see, the structure is the same as page *categories.php*. Nothing new, except for a further call to the database to find the name of the category to which the product is associated, through the $idcategory field. Find the code I'm referring to on lines 271-274. In this way, instead of showing only the *id* of the category, we can make it intelligible to the user by creating a special variable $category_name, row 274, and then showing it inside the table, row 277. Each record (each row of the HTML table) has a command link for *editing* or *deleting* the record, already seen before. We then move on to analyze the HTML form used for adding or modifying a product. Here we will find some new features compared to the form previously used for managing categories. Even if the structure will be the same, by paginating the fields of the form with an appropriate HTML table and keeping the same graphics, we will have to manage different types of data. See the PHP-HTML code of the *formproduct()* function on the following pages:

```php
135   function formproduct() {
136     global $idu, $mysessionid, $strquery, $msg, $connection;
137     global $idproduct, $idcategory, $product_name, $description, $quantity, $price;
138     global $tax,$img;
139   ?>
140   <table width=400 border=0 cellpadding=0 cellspacing=3 bgcolor="#cccccc">
141     <form action="<?php print $PHP_SELF; ?>" method="post" name="form1" enctype="multipart/form-data">
142     <input type="hidden" name="action" value="save">
143     <input type="hidden" name="idproduct" value="<?php print $idproduct; ?>">
144     <input type="hidden" name="idu" value="<?php print $idu; ?>">
145     <input type="hidden" name="mysessionid" value="<?php print $mysessionid; ?>">
146     <input type="hidden" name="img_in_db" value="<?php print $img; ?>">
147     <tr>
148       <td colspan=2 class="ss" align=center><?php print $msg; ?></td>
149     </tr>
150     <tr>
151       <td align=right >Category</td>
152       <td align=left valign=top>
153       <select name="idcategory">
154       <?php
155       $sql = "select * from PHP_course_categories order by category";
156       $result = mysqli_query($connection,$sql) or die(mysqli_error());
157         while ($ValoriRiga = mysqli_fetch_array($result)) {
158           $idcat = $ValoriRiga["idcategory"];
159           $cat = $ValoriRiga["category"];
160       print"<option value=\"$idcat\">$cat";
161       }
162       ?>
163       </select>
164       </td>
165     </tr>
166     <tr>
167       <td align=right >Product Name</td>
168       <td align=left valign=top><input type="text" size="40" maxlength="100" name="product_name" value="<?php
         print $product_name; ?>"></td>
169     </tr>
170     <tr>
171       <td align=right >Image</td>
172       <td align=left valign=top><img src="../img/<?php print "$img";?>" height="50"><br><input type="file"
         name="img" value="<?php print $img; ?>"></td>
173     </tr>
174     <tr>
175       <td align=right>Description</td>
176       <td align=left valign=top><textarea name="description" rows=10 cols=40><?php print $description; ?></
         textarea></td>
177     </tr>
178     <tr>
179       <td align=right>Quantity</td>
180       <td align=left valign=top><input type="text" size="10" maxlength="100" name="quantity" value="<?php
         print $quantity; ?>"></td>
181     </tr>
182     <tr>
183       <td align=right>Price</td>
184       <td align=left valign=top><input type="text" size="5" maxlength="19" name="price" value="<?php print
         $price; ?>"> $</td>
185     </tr>
186     <tr>
187       <td align=right >Tax</td>
188       <td align=left valign=top>
189         <select name="tax">
190           <option value="4" <?php if($tax=="4"){print " selected";}?>>4%
191           <option value="8" <?php if($tax=="8"){print " selected";}?>>8%
192           <option value="20" <?php if($tax=="20"){print " selected";}?>>20%
193         </select>
194       </td>
195     </tr>
196     <tr>
197       <td colspan=2 align=center><input type="submit" name="save" value="Save"></td>
198     </tr>
199     </form>
200     </table>
201   <?php
202   }
203   ################################################################################
```

<!=== Andrea Mauro Raimondi ===>

The first peculiarity is found as an *attribute* of the <form> tag, line 141: *enctype="multipart/form-data"*. This encoding of the transmitted data is necessary when you want to send a file to the server through *post* requests, as in this HTML form. Scrolling through the code, in line 172, you will find an <input type="***file***">, which has the task of making the user choose a file from their computer and upload it to a predefined folder on the server. This folder is defined in the code block of the *switch* that handles the *$action* variable, when it has *value=save*. That is, when the data arrives from the HTML form.

We also find a new field of type <input type="***hidden***">, line 146, which has the function of containing the name of any image associated with the product. We will need it when we want to modify a record without changing the image already associated with the record itself.

Lines 153-163 create a field of type **<select>**, a drop-down menu, which contains the names of the various product categories. It takes as *value*, the *idcategory* field taken from the query made on categories table, rows 155-160, by looping on the result of the query itself. So we have the data of all categories with their id.

Finally, we find a field of type ***<textarea></textarea>***, line 176, which contains the *text* of the product description. It is used in cases where the length of the text that will be inserted is not known and it is assumed that it may be lengthy.

<?php Building Real World PHP Applications ?>

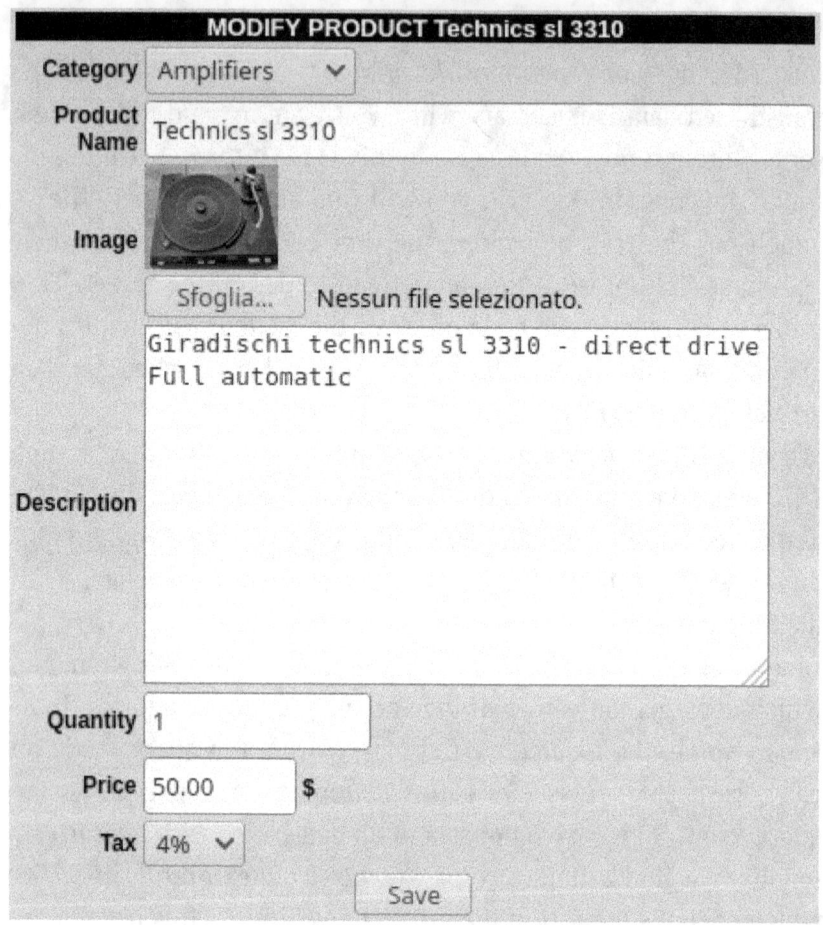

Here is the form for product management in all its beauty.

As we see the category that appears related to this article is not correct. The code found in the previous pages presents a problem: it does not distinguish the category already paired to a product. The following simple change should be made:

{106}

```
159        $cat = $ValoriRiga["category"];
160      print "<option value=\"$idcat\"";
161      if ($idcategory == $idcat) print " selected ";
162      print ">$cat";
163      }
```

In this way, a comparison is made between the variable *$idcate-gory* that contains the eventual value of a category assigned previously, with one of the values retrieved from the database table categories. When the two idcategories are the same, then we proceed to write the selected attribute relating to that <option>.

Here is the form after the modification: notice how now the correct category is displayed.

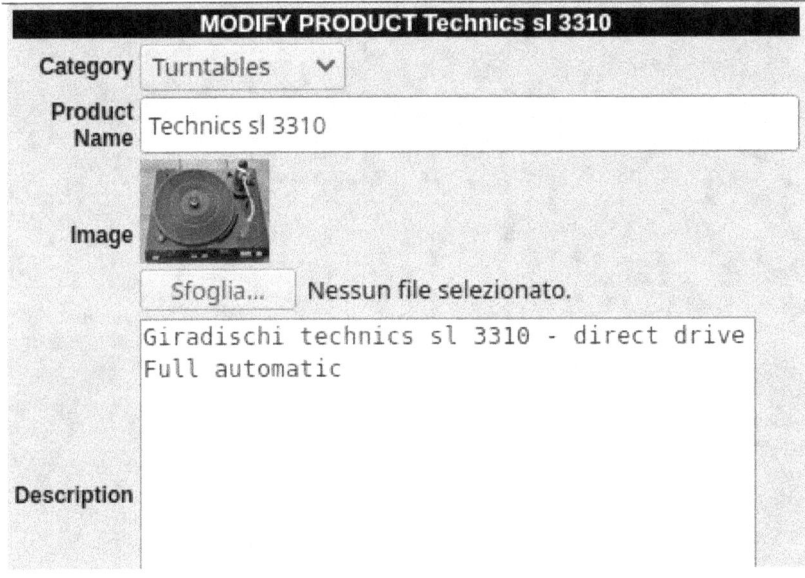

Once you click on "*Save*" button, the data is sent to the server to be processed and entered into the database. The same *products.php* page will be called, and the code block enclosed in the *switch case "save"* will be executed.

```php
66    case "save":
69
70        if (($_FILES['img']['name'] != "")) {
71            $mydate = date("Ymdhs");
72            $uploaddir = '../img/';
73            $userfile_tmp = $_FILES['img']['tmp_name'];
74            $userfile_name = $_FILES['img']['name'];
75            $userfile_name = $mydate." ".$idu." ".$idcategory."L".$userfile_name;
76            $is_img = getimagesize($_FILES['img']['tmp_name']);
77            if (!$is_img) {
78            print "Only image please!";
79            exit;
80            }
81            if (move_uploaded_file($userfile_tmp, $uploaddir . $userfile_name)) {
82                echo "File sended successfully";
83            }else{
84            echo "Upload not valid!";
85            }
86        }
87        else {
88            if ($_REQUEST["img_in_db"] != "")
89            {
90                $userfile_name = $_REQUEST["img_in_db"];
91            }
92        }
93
94        if ($idproduct == "0") { //new product;
95
96            $sql = "INSERT INTO PHP_course_products (idcategory,product_name,description,quantity,price,tax,img)
97                values ('$idcategory','$product_name','$description','$quantity','$price','$tax','$userfile_name')";
98            $result = mysqli_query($connection,$sql);
99            if (! $result)
100           {
101           echo "<b>Record was not added!</b>";
102           }
103           else
104           {
105           echo "Record added.";
106           }
107       }
108       else { //update record;
109           $sql = "UPDATE PHP_course_products SET
110               idcategory='$idcategory',product_name='$product_name',description='$description',
111               quantity='$quantity',price='$price',tax='$tax',img='$userfile_name'
112               WHERE idproduct=$idproduct";
113           $result = mysqli_query($connection,$sql);
114           if (! $result)
115           {
116           echo "<b>Record not updated!</b>";
117           }
118           else
119           {
120           echo "Record modified.";
121           }
122       }
123       //break; // <======= Note the commented line to make sure to perform the default switch code
124 ######################################################################
```

<!=== Andrea Mauro Raimondi ===>

Lines 70-92 manage the upload of the image to the server. The code is enclosed in a block of code, lines 70-86, which is executed if the **img** *form field* is not empty. Notice how we use the superglobal variable *$_FILE['img']['name']*, which is an array of elements uploaded from the PHP page in use. Through it, we access the properties of the uploaded file as *$_FILES['img'] ['tmp_name']*, which contains the name of the temporary file before being saved. Using function *$is_img=**getimagesize**($ _ FILES ['img'] ['tmp_name']);* we can check if the file is of t*ype image* and not of some other type, line 76. We also create some variables that define the name of the file to make it unique, line 75, by adding to it the *user id,* the *idcategory*, and a variable that represents the time per second when the upload took place.

Using the PHP *move_uploaded_file()* function, the file is saved in a folder on the server. This folder was defined in line 72 using variable *$uploaddi*r.

If, on the other hand, the *img form field* is empty, the system checks if the <input hidden="img_in_db"> field contains data. If so, it means that the record had already an image, and therefore its value is assigned to the *$userfile_name* variable. This variable will then be used in queries to save product data in our database table. See lines 96 and 109.

The procedure for checking and saving the image is performed before saving data. For this step we use the same mode seen for the categories: we check the value of the variable *$idproduct* (previously it was *$idcategory*), which is the *unique* field that determines a product in this case or, in general, of the *unique* field of the table you work on. If the value is *zero*, then it is a *new product* to insert and the SQL *INSERT* command is issued, lines 94-107; if, on the other hand, the variable has a value *greater* than zero, then the record is updated, through the *UPDATE* instruction, lines 108-122.

Sure, before entering the data into the database it is possible to perform other checks, such as, for example, checking whether a product with the same name is already present, or whether the price is a numeric data, or even the presence of some fields we may consider mandatory.

In *data control*, we can follow two ways: perform the control on the *client-side*, through javascript functions, before sending the data to the server, or on the *server-side*. From my point of view, *client-side* checks are more easily manipulated by bad-intentioned people or by those who have time to waste, because they may show the logic of the controls performed. While on the *server-side* this does not happen.

Certainly, we can decide to use both methods.

After having seen the *product management*, let's move on to *user management*, that is, who can access the back office area and what can he does.

<!=== Andrea Mauro Raimondi ===>

USERS MANAGEMENT

This back-office area allows you to manage users access to the back-office itself. There are usually two or more access levels: *admin level* and *user level*. Based on the needs of our application, it is possible to create and manage access levels based on what a user can or cannot do (insert, modify, delete a record), can or cannot see or manage: the *user* level, for example, does not see and does not manage the user management area. We have to perform checks on the type of user before displaying certain data or certain links.

In our example, we plan to use two types of users: "*admin*" and "*editor*". The "*editor*" type of user *cannot* manage the users of the application.

These are the menu items that the "*admin*" user sees:

SELECT:

MANAGE USERS

MANAGE CATEGORIES

MANAGE PRODUCTS

LOGOUT

This is the menu for the "*editor*" user type:

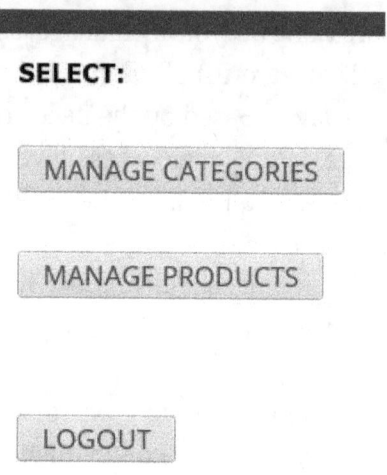

As you can see, in this case, the link to user management is missing: there is no "MANAGE USERS" button.

Here is the code that checks the user type:

```
16    <tr><td><br/><br/></td></tr>
17    <?php
18  ▼ if ($xlevel=="0") {
19    ?>
20    <tr><td><input type="button" onclick="document.location.href='users.php?i
      $idu;?>';" value="MANAGE USERS"></td></tr>
21    <tr><td><br/><br/></td></tr>
22    <?php
23    }
24    ?>
```

It simply evaluates the value of the *$xlevel* variable, which is created in the *utility_inc.php* file. If you remember, this file has the task of verifying the state of the session, through the variables

$idu and *$mysessionid*. The first variable contains the reference to the user who has logged in, in this way, we can retrieve all the data that refer to it, including its level. Having established, by our convention, that the "*admin*" type user has level 0 (zero) and the "*editor*" type user has type "1" level, it is easy to perform the check we are talking about.

Therefore, only an "*admin*" user can view the list of users and perform operations on the relative *PHP_course_user*s table.

This is the user list that appears once you click on the relative menu item.

USERS LIST						
[MENU] [NEW RECORD]						
Name	Username	Active	Level	Access		
Andrea Raimondi	admin	1	Admin	22	[Modify][Delete]	
Antonio Rossi	editor	1	Editor	1	[Modify][Delete]	

On the next page, you will find the structure of the *users.php* file, which deals with managing interactions with the PHP_course_users table. As you can see it is identical of PHP pages already seen previously, apart, of course, the variables and the names of the HTML form fields. In summary, a PHP page in the back-office area in our system has this structure:

- includes HTML header
- retrieving variables of HTML forms or query string
- control value of the *$action* variable with *switch* statement
- create HTML form inside a PHP function
- create HTML table for listing records inside a PHP function
- includes HTML footer

```
6   ?>
7   <?php
8   include('zz top inc.php');
9   include('utility inc.php');
10  $action = $_REQUEST["action"];
11  $iduser = $_REQUEST["iduser"];
12  $name = $_REQUEST["name"];
13  $username = $_REQUEST["username"];
14  $password = $_REQUEST["password"];
15  $active = $_REQUEST["active"];
16  $level = $_REQUEST["level"];
17
18 ▶ switch ($action) {
98  }
99  ?>
100 <?php
101 ########################################
102 ############# form  users ############
103 ########################################
104 ▶ function formuser() {
151  }
152 ########################################
153 #############function list users ######
154 ########################################
155 ▶ function list records() {
226  }
227  ?>
228  <?php
229  //page footer;
230  include('zz bottom inc.php');
231  ?>
```

Let's see, as a review exercise, the detail of this page's code.

<!=== Andrea Mauro Raimondi ===>

The *switch* control group:

```
18  ▼ switch ($action) {
19     ##########################################################################
20     ############## modify record ##########################################
21     ##########################################################################
22     case "modify":
23        $query = "select * from PHP course users where iduser=$iduser";
24        $result = mysqli query($connection,$query) or die(mysqli error());
25  ▼     while ($ValoriRiga = mysqli fetch array($result)) {
26           $iduser = $ValoriRiga["iduser"];
27           $username = $ValoriRiga["username"];
28           $password = $ValoriRiga["password"];
29           $name = $ValoriRiga["name"];
30           $active = $ValoriRiga["active"];
31           $level = $ValoriRiga["level"];
32        }
33        $msg = "MODIFY  USER $name";
34        formuser();
35        break;
36     ##########################################################################
37     ############## delete record ##########################################
38     ##########################################################################
39     case "delete":
40        $sql  = "DELETE FROM PHP course users WHERE iduser=$iduser";
41        $result = mysqli query($connection,$sql);
42        if (! $result)
43  ▼     {
44           echo "<b>The record was not deleted!</b>";
45        }
46        else
47  ▼     {
48           echo "Record deleted.";
49        }
50        list records();
51        break;
52     ##########################################################################
53     ############## add record  ##########################################
54     ##########################################################################
55     case "add":
56        $iduser = "0";
```

The PHP code that is executed when the *$action* variable is equal
to "**modify**" deals with looking for data available in database relating to a single user, identified through the *$iduser* variable. As
you can see, line 23, the *$query* variable is created. It contains the
SQL code to be sent to database. Notice that the *where* clause did
not enclose the *$iduser* variable by single quotes. This does not

generate an error as long as the variable contains a *numeric* value. If for some reason (input error, hacking attempt) the variable is of another type then numeric, the database will return an error. It is therefore always better to put the values of a query between sin- gles quotes. In this case, it would be better to write:

where iduser='$ iduser'.

Once the data has been retrieved from the MySQL table, the PHP code prints the form that will allow the user to manage them.

If, on the other hand, *$action* is equal to "**delete**", the code will execute a *DELETE* query, which has the function of deleting the record from the database. If the operation is successful, the mes- sage "Record deleted" is displayed, line 48, otherwise, the messa- ge "The record was not deleted!", line 44, is displayed, together with the list of records in the table recalled by function *list_re- cord()*.

Both the modification and the deletion of a given record are done through the links highlighted below.

USERS LIST						
[MENU] [NEW RECORD]						
Name	Username	Active	Level	Access		
Andrea Raimondi	admin	1	Admin	22	[Modify][Delete]	
Antonio Rossi	editor	1	Editor	1	[Modify][Delete]	

<!=== Andrea Mauro Raimondi ===>

```
55   case "add":
56       $iduser = "0";
57       $msg = "ADD NEW USER";
58       formuser();
59       break;
60   ############################################################################
61   ###############salva dati###################################################
62   ############################################################################
63   case "save":
64       if ($iduser=="0") { //new user;
65           $sql = "INSERT INTO PHP course users (name,username,password,level,active)
66               values ('$name','$username','$password',$level,$active)";
67           $result = mysqli query($connection,$sql);
68           if (! $result)
69           {
70           echo "<b>Record was not added!</b>";
71           }
72           else
73           {
74           echo "Record added.";
75           }
76       }
77       else { //update record;
78           $sql = "update PHP course users set
79               name='$name',username='$username',password='$password',
80               level='$level',active='$active' where iduser='$iduser'";
81           $result = mysqli query($connection,$sql);
82           if (! $result)
83           {
84           echo "<b>Record not updated!</b>";
85           }
86           else
87           {
88           echo "Record modified.";
89           }
90       }
91       //break; // <======= Note the commented line to make sure to perform the defaul
```

If the *$action* variable has the value "***add***", the application will assign the value 0 (zero) to the *$iduser* variable and will display the HTML form in the browser to create a new user. If the *$action* variable has the value "***save***" it means that data comes from the form. This is the only situation in which the *$action* variable takes the "***save***" value. In this case, as we know, we have two possibilities which are discriminated by the value assumed by the *$iduser* variable. If *$iduser* is equal to 0 (zero) we are in the presence of a new record to insert in a database table. The query will therefore be of type "***INSERT***", line 65. If, on the other hand, *$iduser* is greater than zero, the record is already present in the ta-

ble and it is necessary to *modify* it. We will use the SQL statement
"***UPDATE***", line 78.

```
92    ###############################################################
93    ############## default: list ##################################
94    ###############################################################
95    default:
96        list records();
97        break;
98    }
99    ?>
```

The *switch case* "***default***" occurs if any other conditions fail. In our code, the procedure will display in the browser the list of records of *PHP_course_users* table.

Now, let's see the code of the *formuser()* function which, as we know, displays the HTML form for manage user data.

```
104  function formuser() {
105    global $idu, $mysessionid, $strquery, $msg;
106    global $iduser, $name, $username, $password, $level, $active;
107    ?>
108  <table width=400 border=0 cellpadding=0 cellspacing=3 bgcolor="#cccccc">
109        <form action="<?php print $PHP_SELF; ?>" method="post" name="form1">
110        <input type="hidden" name="action" value="save">
111        <input type="hidden" name="iduser" value="<?php print $iduser; ?>">
112        <input type="hidden" name="idu" value="<?php print $idu; ?>">
113        <input type="hidden" name="mysessionid" value="<?php print $mysessionid; ?>">
114        <tr>
115            <td colspan=2 class="ss" align=center><?php print $msg; ?></td>
116        </tr>
117        <tr>
118          <td align=right >Name</td>
119          <td align=left valign=top>
120              <input type="text" size="40" maxlength="100" name="name" value="<?php print $name; ?>">
121          </td>
122        </tr>
123        <tr>
124          <td align=right >Username</td>
125          <td align=left valign=top>
126              <input type="text" size="40" maxlength="100" name="username" value="<?php print $username; ?>">
127          </td>
128        </tr>
129        <tr>
130          <td align=right >Password</td>
131          <td align=left valign=top>
132              <input type="password" size="40" maxlength="100" name="password" value="<?php print $password; ?>">
133          </td>
134        </tr>
```

We note that in line 110 there is the <input type="hidden"> field with "***save***" value. This will then become the *$action* variable.

<!=== Andrea Mauro Raimondi ===>

```
135   <tr>
136     <td align=right >Active</td>
137     <td align=left valign=top>
138       SI<input type="radio" name="active" value="1" <?php if($active=="1"){print " checked";}?>>
139       NO<input type="radio" name="active" value="0" <?php if($active=="0"){print " checked";}?>>
140     </td>
141   </tr>
142   <tr>
143     <td align=right >Type</td>
144     <td align=left valign=top>
145       <select name="level">
146       <option value="1" <?php if($level=="1"){print " selected";}?>>Editor
147       <option value="0" <?php if($level=="0"){print " selected";}?>>Admin
148       </select>
149     </td>
150   </tr>
151   <tr>
152     <td colspan=2 align=center>
153       <input type="submit" name="save" value="Save">
154     </td>
155   </tr>
156   </form>
157   </table>
158 <?php
159 }
```

We note, lines 138 and 139, a new type of <input>, the type=**radio**, which allows to create mutually exclusive option fields. This happens if all inputs of that type have the same name attribute, that is if we call them with the same name.

By doing so, only one of the options available for that field can be selected by the user.

If, on the other hand, we needed to allow multiple choices, the most suitable type of <input> tag is the one with the **type=checkbox** *attribute* and with the same name attribute for all options:

<input type="checkbox" name="color" value="white">White
<input type="checkbox" name="color" value="red">Red
<input type="checkbox" name="color" value="green">Green
<input type="checkbox" name="color" value="blue">Blue
che visualizzerà:

✓ **White** ☐ **Red** ✓ **Green** ☐ **Blue**

All options are selectable at the same time.

<?php Building Real World PHP Applications ?>

<!=== Andrea Mauro Raimondi ===>

LOGOUT PROCEDURE

When the work-session ends, it is good practice to log-out of the system. In this way, the session variables used will no longer be valid. Any access attempts will be avoided.
To log-out from our application, select the "**LOGOUT**" button in main menu.

SELECT:

MANAGE USERS

MANAGE CATEGORIES

MANAGE PRODUCTS

LOGOUT

This will pass the action to the *logout.php* page.

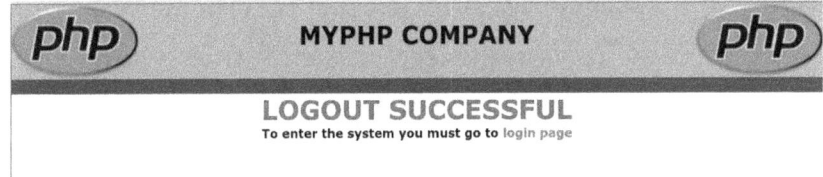

This is logout.php page code:

```php
<?php
$_SESSION["alive"] = "0";
include_once('zz_top_inc.php');
if ($mysessionid!="") {
$today = date("Y-m-d H:i:s",time());
$sql = "UPDATE PHP_course_logutenti_admin SET STATE=0,DATALOGOUT='$today' WHERE SESSIONID='$mysessionid'";
$result = mysqli_query($connection,$sql);
//print $sql;
$idu = 0;
}
print "<font color=\"#cc0000\" size=\"+2\">LOGOUT SUCCESSFUL </font> <br>
      To enter the system you must go to <a href=\"login.php\">login page</a>";
include('zz_bottom_inc.php');
exit;
?>
```

As we see, lines 11-15, table *PHP_course_loutenti_admin* that keeps track of sessions is updated, setting the **STATE** field to 0 (zero) and updating the *logout date* with the current date per second. To do this, we create a variable, *$today*, which will contain this date value, employing the PHP *date()* function. We also proceed to set the variable *$idu* to zero.

If we remember *utility_inc.php* file, it performed a check on the **STATE** field and the **$idu** variable. Here it is for convenience.

```php
<?php
$idu = $_REQUEST["idu"];
$mysessionid = $_REQUEST["mysessionid"];

$strquery = "idu=$idu&mysessionid=$mysessionid";
if ($mysessionid == "") {
    $idu = 0;
}
else {
    $sql = "select * from PHP_course_logutenti_admin
            WHERE SESSIONID='$mysessionid' AND STATE='1'";
    $resultbl = mysqli_query($connection,$sql) or die(mysqli_error());
    $sesistel=mysqli_num_rows($resultbl);
    if ($sesistel > 0) {
    $sqlb = "SELECT * FROM PHP_course_users WHERE iduser=$idu AND active='1'";
    $resultb = mysqli_query($connection,$sqlb) or die(mysqli_error());
    $ValoriRigab1 = mysqli_fetch_array($resultb);
    $xlevel = $ValoriRigab1["level"];
    $xname = $ValoriRigab1["name"];
    }
    else {
        $idu = 0;
    }
}
if ($idu == 0) {
    include_once('zz_top_inc.php');
    print "<font color=\"#cc0000\" size=\"+3\">SESSION EXPIRED!</font><br>";
    print "You need to <a href=\"login.php\">login</a>";
    include('zz_bottom_inc.php');
    exit;
    }
```

<!=== Andrea Mauro Raimondi ===>

PUBLIC AREA: WEBSITE

After entering categories and products through the back-office area, we are ready to show them to the public through a website. We will create a simple home page that will shows the list of categories and, once you have chosen a category, we will see the related products. To transform this simple "showcase" site in something more complex, just add the cart, the checkout, and payment procedure, and we have a real ecommerce (details in Volume 2). This is the home page.

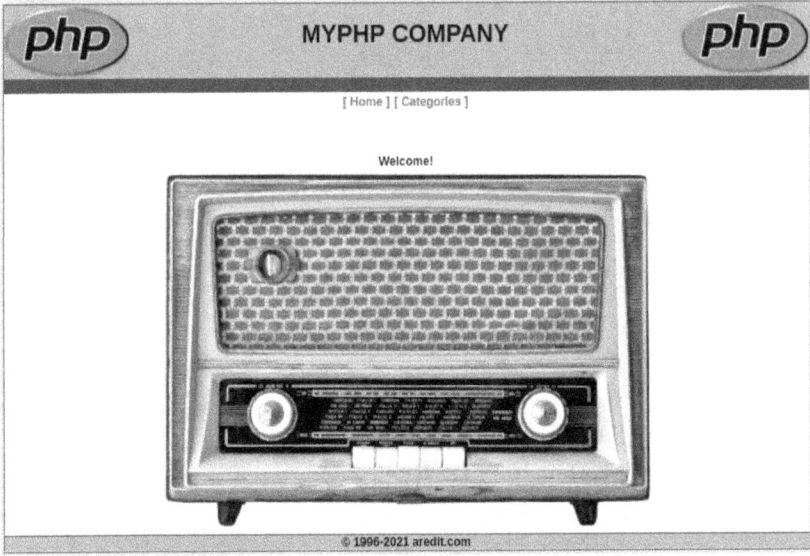

The entire "public" part of our application is located in the "*public*" folder, to reach it you must follow this link:
https://www.aredit.com/public/PHPcourse/catalog/public/

<?php Building Real World PHP Applications ?>

The "public" folder contains the following files.

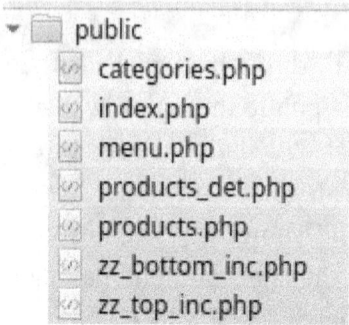

As you can see, the *database connection file* is missing: it will be included, taking it from the *admin* folder. In this way, if we need to move the database to another server, we only need to change the *connection data in one file*.

The *index.php* file has this structure:

```
 6   ?>
 7   <?php
 8   include('zz_top_inc.php');
 9   ?>
10   |
11   <br><br><br>Welcome!<br>
12   <a href="categories.php"><img src="../img/vintageradio.jpeg" width=""></a>
13
14   <?php
15   //footer della pagina;
16   include('zz_bottom_inc.php');
17   ?>
18
```

We find two inclusion files *zz_top_inc.php*, which defines the site header valid for all pages, and *zz_bottom_inc.php* which defines the footer for all pages, with copyright data, in this case. The *body* of the file contains, in addition to the welcome text, a clickable image that link the visitor to categories list.

Let's see in detail the files included.

```
 7 | <!doctype html>
 8   <html>
 9   <head>
10 | <title>...::: MY COMPANY| :::...</title>
11   <meta http-equiv="Content-type" content="text/html; charset=iso-8859-1">
12   <meta name="author" content="Andrea Raimondi - info--AT--aredit.com">
13   <meta name="editor" content="Andrea Raimondi">
14   <meta name="robots" content="noindex">
15   <link rel="shortcut icon" href="../img/favicon.ico" />
16   <link rel=StyleSheet href="../css/73160000.css" type="text/css" media=screen>
17 ▼ <style type="text/css">
18   a:link { color: #ff0000; }
19   a:active { color: #FFCC00; }
20   a:visited { color: #FF0000; }
21   </style></head>
22   <?php
23   include_once('../admin/connection_inc.php');
24   ?>
25   <body>
26   <center>
27 ▼ <table border=1 cellpadding=0 cellspacing=0 bgcolor="#ffffff">
28   <tr>
29   <td>
30 ▼ <table cellspacing=0 cellpadding=0 border=0 width="760" bgcolor="#9999cc">
31       <tr>
32       <td valign=top><img src="../img/php.gif" border=0 align=absmiddle></td>
33       <td valign=top align=center><h1>MYPHP COMPANY</h1></td>
34       <td valign=top align=right><img src="../img/php.gif" border=0 align=absmiddle></td>
35       </tr>
36   <tr bgcolor="#333366"><td colspan="3" height=10> </td></tr>
37   </table>
38 ▼ <table cellspacing=0 cellpadding=0 border=0 width="100%">
39   <tr>
40   <td valign=top align=center height=400>
41   <?php
42   include_once('menu.php');
43   ?>
```

The *zz_top_inc.php* code creates the main HTML table, includes the connection file taken from the admin folder, and includes the file containing the HTML code for the menu, valid for all pages. Keeping the menu items in a separate file saves a lot of time when one wants to change the graphics of the site or the menu items.

In our example, the *menu.php* file simply contains an HTML table with the menu items.

```
1  <table>
2    <tr>
3    <td><a href="./">[ Home ]</a></td>
4    <td><a href="categories.php">[ Categories ]</a></td>
5    </tr>
6  </table>
7
```

menu.php

zz_bottom_inc.php

Once on the home page, the visitor may click the "categories" link, then select a category, and view the products associated with it, to finish with the detail of the chosen product.

Here is the list of categories. As we will notice, the public website of an application like this must show the **contents** of the database. So we use *SELECT* SQL instruction.

Let's see the code in categories.php file, that generates the list of categories.

<!=== Andrea Mauro Raimondi ===>

```php
 7   <?php
 8   include('zz_top_inc.php');
 9   ?>
10   <table cellpadding=2 cellspacing=2 border=0>
11   <tr><td height=20><h2>CATEGORIES</h2></td></tr>
12   <?php
13
14   $sql = "select * from PHP_course_categories order by category";
15
16   $result = mysqli_query($connection,$sql) or die (mysqli_error());
17
18   while ($ValoriRiga = mysqli_fetch_array($result)) {
19
20     $idcategory = $ValoriRiga["idcategory"];
21     $category = $ValoriRiga["category"];
22
23     print "<tr><td><a href=\"products.php?idcat=$idcategory\">$category</a></td></tr>";
24   }
25   ?>
26   </table>
27   <?php
28   //footer della pagina:
29   include('zz_bottom_inc.php');
30   ?>
```

The *$sql* variable contains the SQL command to be sent to the database: it searches all the data contained in the *PHP_course_categories* table and orders them by *category* name.

If the **sort type** is not specified, it will be of *ascending type*. This means, in the case of sorting for a numeric field, from the lowest to the highest number. If the field is of the string type (char, varchar) the sorting will be alphabetical, from A to Z. Otherwise we can sort the records found in *descending order* using the 'DESC' command.

In this case, the SQL statement would become:

select * from PHP_course_categories order by category DESC

The *sort commands* are **ASC**, which is also the default, and **DESC** and always follow the *ORDER BY clause*, after indicating the field to be sorted.

Let's see the effects of the new sorting:

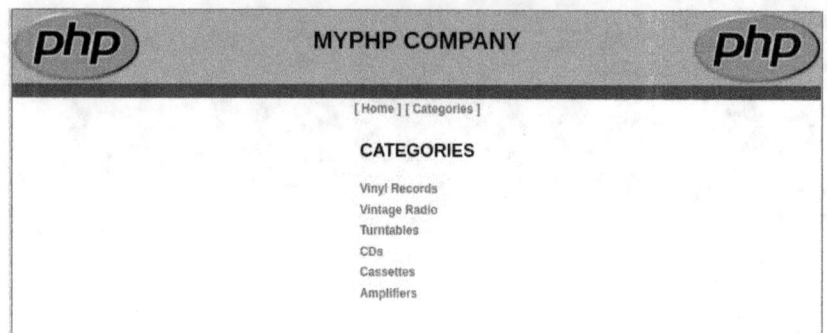

As you can see, the list is in reverse alphabetical order, from Z to A. The link leads to the *products.php* page, passing in the query-string the variable *idcat* which indicates the *category of products* to be displayed, through the **id** taken from the database table.

```
6    ?>
7    <?php
8    include('zz_top_inc.php');
9
10   $idcat = $_REQUEST["idcat"];
11
12   $sql = "select * from PHP_course_categories WHERE idcategory='$idcat'";
13   $result = mysqli_query($connection,$sql) or die (mysqli_error());
14   $ValoriRiga = mysqli_fetch_array($result);
15   $category = strtoupper($ValoriRiga["category"]);
16
17   ?>
```

The *idcat* variable of the querystring will then be combined with a PHP variable *$idcat,* as seen in line 10 of PHP page, *products.-php.*

Lines 12-16 retrieve the category name from the database and then display it in the <table> HTML as a header, line 19:

```
18   <table cellpadding=2 cellspacing=2 border=0>
19     <tr><td height=20 colspan="2" align="center">PRODUCTS FOR CATEGORY <?php print "$category";?></td></tr>
20     <?php
```

<!=== **Andrea Mauro Raimondi** ===>

The code continues by retrieving the products from the *PHP_course_products* database table, selecting them by *category*, using the SQL, **WHERE** clause, line 22. The records found are displayed within the <table>, one record per row.

```
18  <table cellpadding=2 cellspacing=2 border=0>
19  <tr><td height=20 colspan="2" align="center">PRODUCTS FOR CATEGORY <?php print "$category";?></td></tr>
20  <?php
21
22  $sql = "select * from PHP_course_products where idcategory='$idcat' order by product_name";
23  $result = mysqli_query($connection,$sql) or die (mysqli_error());
24  $tot = mysqli_num_rows($result);
25  while ($ValoriRiga = mysqli_fetch_array($result)) {
26  $idproduct = $ValoriRiga["idproduct"];
27  $product_name = $ValoriRiga["product_name"];
28  $img = $ValoriRiga["img"];
29  print "<tr><td><img src=\"../img/$img\" width=\"150\"></td><td><a href=\"products_det.php?
    idprod=$idproduct\">$product_name</a></td></tr>";
30  }
31  ?>
32  </table>
33  <?php
34  include('zz_bottom_inc.php');
35  ?>
```

Here is the result in a browser of the code just analyzed.

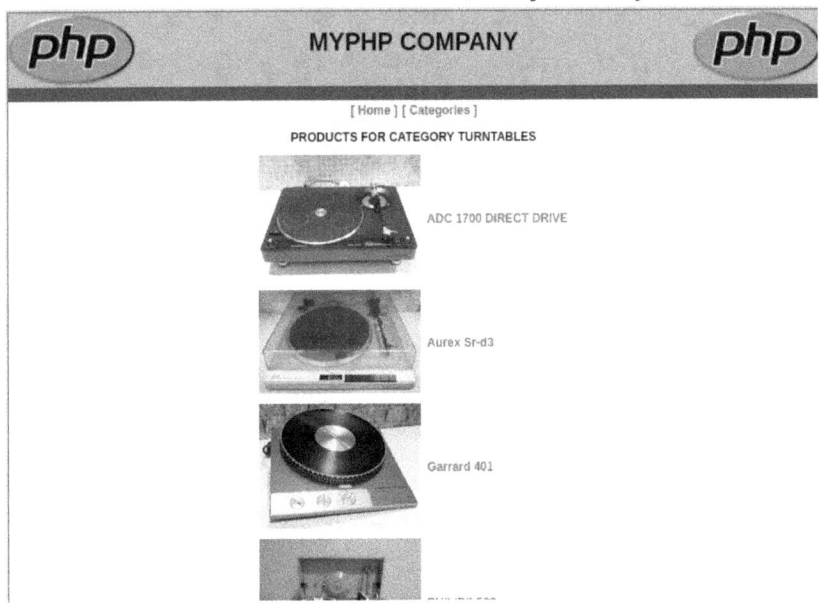

Our visitor can select a product by clicking on the product name, line 29. We can also decide to make product's image clickable. For this you must add the <a> </a> tag to the <img> image tag:

```
27    $product_name = $ValoriRiga["product_name"];
28    $img = $ValoriRiga["img"];
29    print "<tr><td><a href=\"products_det.php?idprod=$idproduct\"><img src=\"../img/$img\" width=\"150\"></a></
~     td><td><a href=\"products_det.php?idprod=$idproduct\">$product_name</a></td></tr>";
```

By click the image the visitor enter the single product's detail page. Here it is in all its vintage beauty:

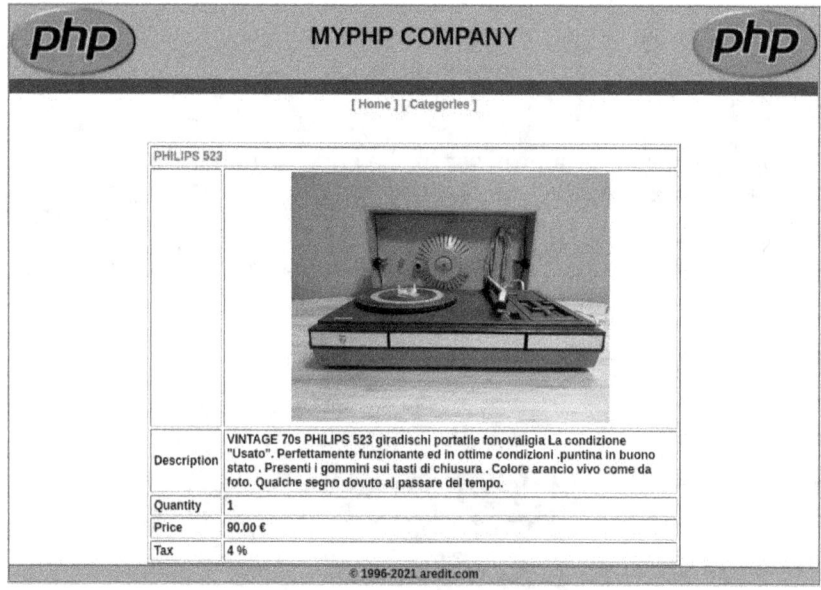

As highlighted by the table border, the page's structure is composed of a two columns <table>. So each <tr> </tr> row will have two <td> </td>, allowing you to view the fields of *PHP_course_products* table.

{130}

<!=== Andrea Mauro Raimondi ===>

Here is the HTML code of *products_det.php*:

```php
    include('zz_top_inc.php');

    $idprod = $_REQUEST['idprod'];
    ?>
    <br><br>
    <table cellpadding=2 cellspacing=2 border=1 width=500>
    <?php

    $sql = "SELECT * FROM PHP_course_products WHERE idproduct='$idprod'";
    $result = mysqli_query($connection,$sql) or die (mysqli_error());
19  while ($ValoriRiga = mysqli_fetch_array($result)) {
    $idproduct = $ValoriRiga["idproduct"];
    $idcategory = $ValoriRiga["idcategory"];
    $product_name = $ValoriRiga["product_name"];
    $description = $ValoriRiga["description"];
    $quantity = $ValoriRiga["quantity"];
    $price = $ValoriRiga["price"];
    $tax = $ValoriRiga["tax"];
    $img = $ValoriRiga["img"];

    print "<tr><td colspan=2><a href=\"products.php?idcat=$idcategory\">$product_name</a></td></tr>";
    print "<tr><td></td><td align=\"center\"><img src=\"../img/$img\" width=\"300\"></td></tr>";
    print "<tr><td width=40>Description</td><td>$description</td></tr>";
    print "<tr><td>Quantity</td><td>$quantity</td></tr>";
    print "<tr><td>Price</td><td>$price &euro;</td></tr>";
    print "<tr><td>Tax</td><td>$tax %</td></tr>";

    }
    ?>
    </table>
    <?php
    //footer
    include('zz_bottom_inc.php');
    ?>
```

The SQL statement is a **SELECT** that searches for the record by its **ID**, *idproduct*. Field's values are then assigned to the related PHP variables. In this case, we could have avoided using the *while loop*, as we are sure to get a single record from the query. In any case, to speed up the writing of an application, it is quicker to copy and paste the code which can work well in all cases of data extraction from a table, beyond the number of records.

<?php Building Real World PHP Applications ?>

Programming is a technique.
Write applications,
think about them,
find solutions
is an art

<!=== Andrea Mauro Raimondi ===>

PART II

Reusing PHP code

<?php Building Real World PHP Applications ?>

During the life of a web application, needs may change, both from the point of view of *functionality* and *graphics*. In the *first case*, it is a question of implementing new PHP and HTML code to the existing one, possibly modifying or adding database tables. In the *second case*, it is a question of modifying the existing HTML code. An application like the one we have developed and described in this book, can have many improvements in functionality: we can turn it into an e-commerce site or an auction site or a blog: add related components and modules such as a shopping cart, a system of payment, visitor interaction forms, comment forms, acquire customer data. We will concentrate in this second part on modifications from the graphic point of view, to make it closer to the current taste. This procedure may require the intervention of a graphic designer specialized on the web, who will provide the new HTML code and related CSS and any javascript code. Or we can find graphic resources on the web, to buy or for free. We choose the second hypothesis and search for "*free HTML 5 templates*". We need templates for both the public website and for the back-office area. See, on the next page, the result in February 2021 regarding this research. The research can take a long time, especially in evaluating if the proposed graphics and the page's structure fit our needs and tastes.

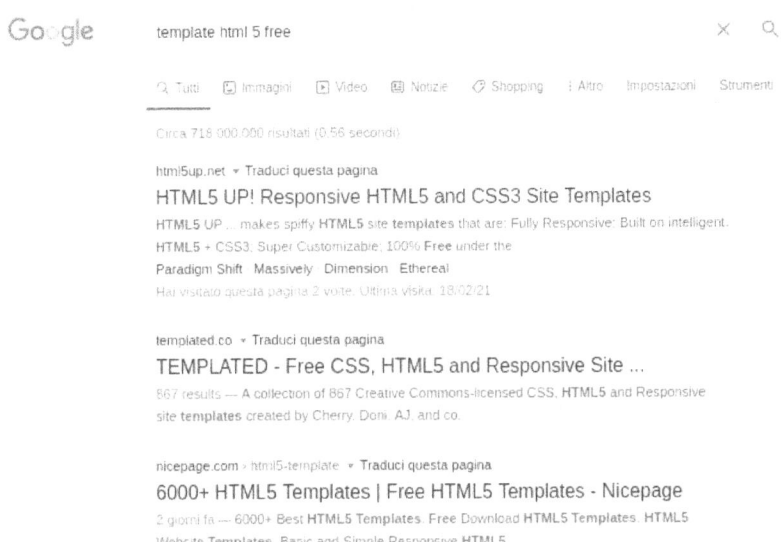

After some checks, we decided to use the theme provided by *https://template-mo.com* for the public part of the application and for the back-office part *https://adminlte.io/*

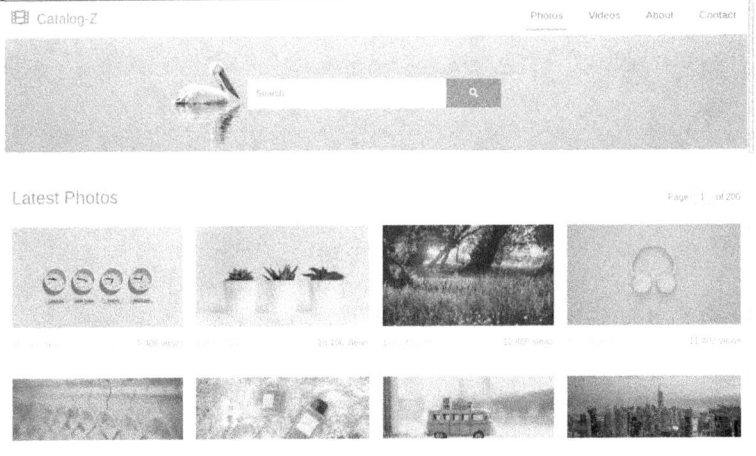

back-office new template:

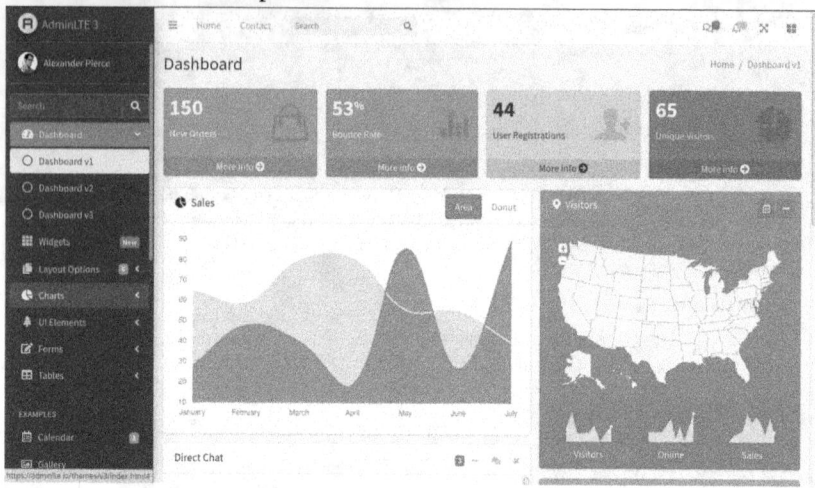

Now it's a matter of adapting the templates' HTML code, making it dynamic using PHP.

After downloading the templates and unpacking the .zip files, we copy the folders to our workspace and proceed with uploading the files to the web server.

<!=== **Andrea Mauro Raimondi** ===>

NEW WEBSITE GRAPHICS

For the website part, we keep the same functionalities: list of product categories, list of products in a given category, and product detail.

Looking at the code of the various template's HTML pages, we notice that it is divided between main areas: one for the header, one for the content of the page, and one for the footer.

```
<!DOCTYPE html>
<html lang="en">
<head>
    <meta charset="UTF-8">
    <meta name="viewport" content="width=device-width, initial-scale=1.0">
    <title>Catalog-Z About page</title>
    <link rel="stylesheet" href="css/bootstrap.min.css">
    <link rel="stylesheet" href="fontawesome/css/all.min.css">
    <link rel="stylesheet" href="css/templatemo-style.css">
</head>
<body>
    <!-- Page Loader -->
    <div id="loader-wrapper">
        <div id="loader"></div>
        <div class="loader-section section-left"></div>
        <div class="loader-section section-right"></div>
    </div>
    <nav class="navbar navbar-expand-lg">
        <div class="container-fluid">
            <a class="navbar-brand" href="index.html">
                <i class="fas fa-film mr-2"></i>
                Catalog-Z
            </a>
            <button class="navbar-toggler" type="button" data-toggle="collapse" data-
target="#navbarSupportedContent" aria-controls="navbarSupportedContent" aria-expanded="false" aria-
label="Toggle navigation">
                <i class="fas fa-bars"></i>
            </button>
            <div class="collapse navbar-collapse" id="navbarSupportedContent">
                <ul class="navbar-nav ml-auto mb-2 mb-lg-0">
                    <li class="nav-item">
                </ul>
            </div>
        </div>
    </nav>

    <div class="tm-hero d-flex justify-content-center align-items-center" data-parallax="scroll" data-image-
src="img/hero.jpg"></div>

    <div class="container-fluid tm-mt-60">
        <div class="row mb-4">
            <h2 class="col-12 tm-text-primary">
                About Catalog-Z Website Template
            </h2>
        </div>
        <div class="row tm-mb-74 tm-row-1640">
            <div class="col-lg-5 col-md-6 col-12 mb-3">
                <img src="img/about.jpg" alt="Image" class="img-fluid">
            </div>
            <div class="col-lg-7 col-md-6 col-12">
                <div class="tm-about-img-text">
                    <p class="mb-4">
You may support TemplateMo website by making <a href="https://paypal.me/templatemo"
target="_parent" rel="sponsored">a small contribution</a> via PayPal. This will be helpful for
us. We hope you like this Catalog-Z photo / video template for your website. We are making new
templates regularly for you. Please come back and visit our <a rel="sponsored" href="https://
templatemo.com" target="_parent">TemplateMo website</a> again. </p>
                    <p>
Credits go to Pexels and Unsplash for photos and video used in this template. Catalog-Z
is free <a rel="sponsored" href="https://v5.getbootstrap.com/">Bootstrap 5</a> Alpha 2
HTML Template designed for video and photo websites.</p>
```

<?php **Building Real World PHP Applications** ?>

```
129          </div>
130      </div> <!-- container-fluid, tm-container-content -->
131
132  ▼  <footer class="tm-bg-gray pt-5 pb-3 tm-text-gray tm-footer">
133  ▼      <div class="container-fluid tm-container-small">
134  ▼          <div class="row">
135  ▼              <div class="col-lg-6 col-md-12 col-12 px-5 mb-5">
136                      <h3 class="tm-text-primary mb-4 tm-footer-title">About Catalog-Z</h3>
137                      <p>Catalog-Z is free Bootstrap 5 Alpha 2 HTML Template for video and photo websites. You can
                         freely use this TemplateMo layout for a front-end integration with any kind of CMS
                         website.</p>
138                  </div>
139  ▼              <div class="col-lg-3 col-md-6 col-sm-6 col-12 px-5 mb-5">
140  ▼                  <h3 class="tm-text-primary mb-4 tm-footer-title">Our Links</h3>
141  ▼                  <ul class="tm-footer-links pl-0">
142                          <li><a href="#">Advertise</a></li>
143                          <li><a href="#">Support</a></li>
144                          <li><a href="#">Our Company</a></li>
145                          <li><a href="#">Contact</a></li>
146                      </ul>
147                  </div>
```

Up to line 47, we find the code of the *header*, which is repeated on every page. Lines 48-132 form the central part of the page, where we will insert the content. The page *footer* starts from line 132. With version 5 of HTML, *new TAGs* have been introduced that define the layout, such as <footer></footer> or <nav></nav>, which defines an area for the header or menu. It will become natural to look for repetitions in the code and find ways to avoid them. In this case, it is almost natural to create a file for the header and one for the footer.

We are essentially repeating what we have already done for the first version of the application, creating two files that we will call zz_top.php and zz_footer.php. We will also create a "*template*" file to be used for the various pages of the site and which will include the other two files.

The logic when creating files to include that represent parts of a web page, is to search for elements common to all pages (or to as many pages as possible). In this way, for any further changes, it will be enough to intervene on a single file. It is necessary to learn how to find similarities and differences in an HTML structure, as in this case.

<!=== Andrea Mauro Raimondi ===>

We note in *zz_top.php* file, shown below, the addition of the *connection_inc.php* connection file, located in the *admin* folder, line 11.

```
1   <!DOCTYPE html>
2   <html lang="en">
3   <head>
4       <meta charset="UTF-8">
5       <meta name="viewport" content="width=device-width, in:
6       <title>AREdit.com = PHP Course</title>
7       <link rel="stylesheet" href="css/bootstrap.min.css">
8       <link rel="stylesheet" href="fontawesome/css/all.min.(
9       <link rel="stylesheet" href="css/templatemo-style.css'
10   <?php
11   include('../admin/connection_inc.php');
12   global $connection;
13   ?>
14   </head>
15   <body>
16       <!-- Page Loader -->
17       <div id="loader-wrapper">
18           <div id="loader"></div>
19
20           <div class="loader-section section-left"></div>
21           <div class="loader-section section-right"></div>
22
23       </div>
24       <nav class="navbar navbar-expand-lg">
25           <div class="container-fluid">
26               <a class="navbar-brand" href="index.php">
27                   <i class="fas fa-film mr-2"></i>
28                   MyPHP Company
29               </a>
```

We note on lines 7-9 the CSS files included in the project. The development of the web, thanks to the increase in the speed of connections and available devices, has led to the expansion of the capabilities of browsers and systems connected to them, improving graphic and functional capabilities. This has led to a strong development in the use of CSS and javascript. Is now possible to create HTML code that can be used simultaneously on devices with screens of different sizes. Simplifying the construction of the pages, with the introduction of new HTML tags, as mentioned in precedence. This has led, among other things, to a massive use, in pages' construction, of the <DIV> </DIV> tag, whose appearance and behavior is governed by the CSS classes, imposed on it, as can be seen by studying the code HTML of these new pages. Here is the final part of the *zz_footer.php* file:

```
19        <li class="mb-2"><a href="https://facebook.com"><i class="fab fa-facebook"></i></a><
20        <li class="mb-2"><a href="https://twitter.com"><i class="fab fa-twitter"></i></a></l
21        <li class="mb-2"><a href="https://instagram.com"><i class="fab fa-instagram"></i></a
          li>
22        <li class="mb-2"><a href="https://pinterest.com"><i class="fab fa-pinterest"></i></a
          li>
23      </ul>
24      <a href="#" class="tm-text-gray text-right d-block mb-2">Terms of Use</a>
25      <a href="#" class="tm-text-gray text-right d-block">Privacy Policy</a>
26    </div>
27  </div>
28  <div class="row">
29    <div class="col-lg-8 col-md-7 col-12 px-5 mb-3">
30      Copyright 2020 <a href="https://www.aredit.com">AREdit.com</a>.  All rights reserved.
31    </div>
32    <div class="col-lg-4 col-md-5 col-12 px-5 text-right">
33      Designed by <a href="https://templatemo.com" class="tm-text-gray" rel="sponsored"
          target="_blank">TemplateMo</a><br>
34      Modified by <a href="https://www.aredit.com" class="tm-text-gray" rel="sponsored"
          target="_blank">Andrea Raimondi</a>
35    </div>
36  </div>
37  </div>
38  </footer>
39
40  <script src="js/plugins.js"></script>
41  <script>
42      $(window).on("load", function() {
43          $('body').addClass('loaded');
44      });
45  </script>
46  </body>
47  </html>
```

In this case, there are no PHP code additions. Note, however, the inclusion, through the <script> </script> tags, of the javascript files and functions. In templates, you will often find javascript files included at the end of the page. These usually (in 2021) use javascript libraries, that is, a set of javascript functions that, interacting with each other, allow you to obtain effects or functionality

<!=== Andrea Mauro Raimondi ===>

of HTML elements, otherwise available only by writing a lot of javascript and CSS code. The most used at the moment is JQuery. The advice, especially if you are a beginner, is to look for templates as close to what you want your application to be and to appear, to avoid touching both the CSS files and the javascript code. In our case, the PHP code will mostly be added in files that have an interaction with the database. Here is the structure of the new public folder, where you can see both the original .html files and the new .php files:

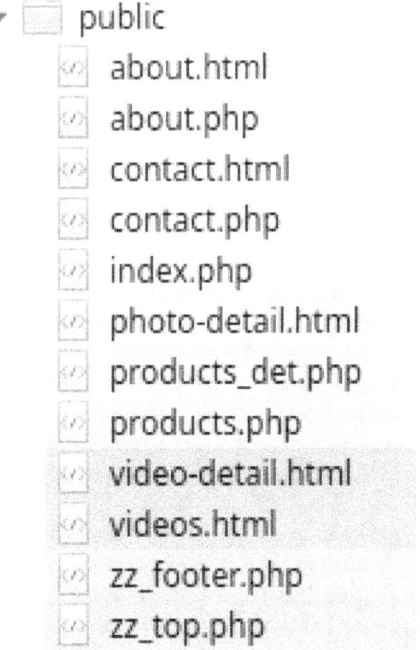

public
about.html
about.php
contact.html
contact.php
index.php
photo-detail.html
products_det.php
products.php
video-detail.html
videos.html
zz_footer.php
zz_top.php

For our new web app, we do not need all the HTML files available in the template we have chosen, so some files will not have the corresponding *.php* file. The main files are the same as the original application: *index.php, products.php, products_det.php*. We have kept other new template's file and transformed it into PHP files just to maintain template consistency, such as about.php and contact.php. Here's what the new home page looks now.

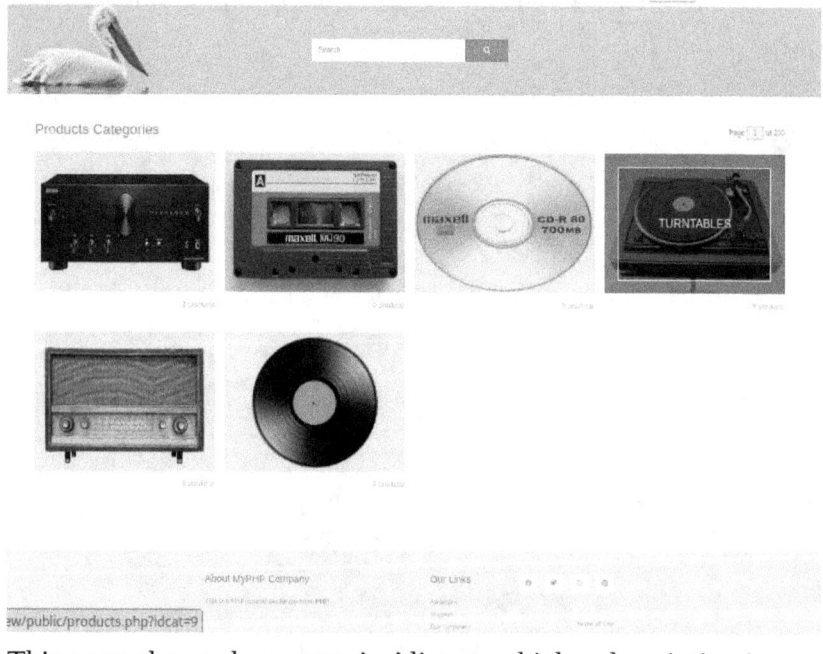

This page shows the categories' list, to which a descriptive image has been combined. To do this, a field has been added to database table that contains the data relating to categories and some PHP code has been added to allow users in back office area to manage it, as we will see later. The search among products in database has

<!=== **Andrea Mauro Raimondi** ===>

also been activated, using the form present in new template's header. Here is *index.php* code

```php
<?php
include("zz_top.php");
?>
<div class="container-fluid tm-container-content tm-mt-60">
        <div class="row mb-4">
            <h2 class="col-6 tm-text-primary">
                Products Categories
            </h2>
            <div class="col-6 d-flex justify-content-end align-items-center">
                <form action="" class="tm-text-primary">
                    Page <input type="text" value="1" size="1" class="tm-input-paging tm-text-primary"
                </form>
            </div>
        </div>
        <div class="row tm-mb-90 tm-gallery">

        <?php

        $sql = "select * from PHP_course_categories order by category ASC";

        $result = mysqli_query($connection,$sql) or die (mysqli_error());

        while ($ValoriRiga = mysqli_fetch_array($result)) {

        $idcategory = $ValoriRiga["idcategory"];
        $category = $ValoriRiga["category"];
        $img = $ValoriRiga["img"];

        $sql2 = "SELECT * FROM PHP_course_products WHERE idcategory='$idcategory'";
        $result2 = mysqli_query($connection,$sql2) or die (mysqli_error());
        $total_products = mysqli_num_rows($result2);
        ?>
            <div class="col-xl-3 col-lg-4 col-md-6 col-sm-6 col-12 mb-5">
                <figure class="effect-ming tm-video-item">
                    <img src="../../img/<?php print "$img";?>" alt="Image" class="img-fluid">
                    <figcaption class="d-flex align-items-center justify-content-center">
                        <h2><?php print "$category";?></h2>
                        <a href="products.php?idcat=<?php print "$idcategory";?>">View more</a>
                    </figcaption>
                </figure>
                <div class="d-flex justify-content-between tm-text-gray">
                    <span class="tm-text-gray-light"> </span>
                    <span><?php print "$total_products";?> products</span>
                </div>
            </div>
        <?php
        }
        ?>
        </div> <!-- row -->
            <!-- <div class="row tm-mb-90">
                <div class="col-12 d-flex justify-content-between align-items-center tm-paging-col">
                    <a href="javascript:void(0);" class="btn btn-primary tm-btn-prev mb-2 disabled">Pr
                    <div class="tm-paging d-flex">
                        <a href="javascript:void(0);" class="active tm-paging-link">1</a>
                        <a href="javascript:void(0);" class="tm-paging-link">2</a>
                        <a href="javascript:void(0);" class="tm-paging-link">3</a>
                        <a href="javascript:void(0);" class="tm-paging-link">4</a>
                    </div>
                    <a href="javascript:void(0);" class="btn btn-primary tm-btn-next">Next Page</a>
                </div>
            </div> -->
    </div> <!-- container-fluid, tm-container-content -->
    <?php
    include("zz_footer.php");
    ?>
```

Header code block and footer code block have been removed from the original file, replaced by the PHP file inclusions.

Elements that contained the images of the original file have been deleted, keeping only one as a template, shown on lines 33-45. Some of the HTML code that was not needed has been commented out, lines 50-61. At this point all that remains is to add the PHP code, fetching it from the old file. The only difference is the addition of the *img* field, which contains the image relating to the product category and a *query*, lines 29-31, to obtain each category's products' number, to be displayed under the image, line 43. For this purpose, we used the PHP function *mysqli_num_rows()*, which takes the result of a query as an argument and returns the number of records of the query itself. With the *while* loop in line 23, we get the list of records, in this case, the categories, and display and formatting them as set up by the template.

As can be seen from the image of the home page, when the mouse pointer is positioned on a category, them category's name appears and the image becomes clickable. We do not know anything about this effect, obtained with CSS, at the moment, and we can also avoid knowing it, unless we have to intervene to modify the effect itself or in the event of a malfunction. Explanation of advanced CSS is beyond the scope of this book, so we are content to verify this effect works.

By clicking on the category image, the list of related products is displayed: it is *products.php* file that we had created in older version.

<!=== Andrea Mauro Raimondi ===>

7 products

Note the number of existing products for the "*Turntables*" category.

As we can see from web page's image relating to product's list in the "Turntables" category, graphically, it is similar to the list of categories we saw for the home page. We just replace the query, searching no longer in *PHP_course_categories* table, but *PHP_course_products* table.

In this case, however, let's see how to use a piece of PHP code that makes the database call, dynamically changing the query used.

We have decided to use the *search form* present in the template, to allow site visitors to carry out direct searches among our products.

```php
1    <?php
2    include("zz_top.php");
3
4    $idcat = $_REQUEST["idcat"];
5    $search = $_REQUEST["search"];
6
7    if ($idcat != "") {
8        $sql = "select * from PHP_course_categories WHERE idcategory='$idcat'";
9        $result = mysqli_query($connection,$sql) or die (mysqli_error());
10       $ValoriRiga = mysqli_fetch_array($result);
11       $category = strtoupper($ValoriRiga["category"]);
12
13       $sql = "select * from PHP_course_products where idcategory='$idcat' order by product_name";
14
15   }
16   if ($search != "") {
17
18       $sql = "select * from PHP_course_products where product_name like '%$search%' order by product_name";
19
20   }
21   ?>
22   <div class="container-fluid tm-container-content tm-mt-60">
23       <div class="row mb-4">
24           <h2 class="col-6 tm-text-primary">
25               Products for <?php print "$category";?>
26           </h2>
27           <div class="col-6 d-flex justify-content-end align-items-center">
28               <form action="" class="tm-text-primary">
29                   Page <input type="text" value="1" size="1" class="tm-input-paging tm-text-primary"> of 200
30               </form>
31           </div>
32       </div>
33       <div class="row tm mb 00 tm gallery">
```

Let's analyze the initial code of *products.php*, after the usual inclusion of *zz_top.php*, we retrieve the value of two variables from the query string: one corresponds to *category ID* that comes from category image's link on the home page. The other variable represents the <input> field value of the form that we find on all pages because it is located in the *zz_top.php* file.

```php
49   <div class="tm-hero d-flex justify-content-center align-items-center" data-parallax="scroll" data-image-
     src="img/hero.jpg">
50       <form class="d-flex tm-search-form" method="post" action="products.php">
51           <input class="form-control tm-search-input" name="search" type="search" placeholder="Search" aria-
             label="Search">
52           <button class="btn btn-outline-success tm-search-btn" type="submit">
53               <i class="fas fa-search"></i>
54           </button>
55       </form>
56   </div>
```

Highlight the *name* attribute of <input> tag that belongs to the <form> tag of *zz_top.php* file.

<!=== **Andrea Mauro Raimondi** ===>

From line 7 to line 20 there are two "if" *conditional structures*.
The first, line 7 to line 15, checks if the *$idcat* variable is not empty. If it is not, we first look in *PHP_course_categories* table for the category name and assign it to the *$category* variable. It will be used in the rest of the page to display the the displayed products' category, line 25. We then create variable *$sql* which contains the SQL statement to be sent to database to get the re-cordset with the products' list, line 13.

Second if statement checks if *$search* variable is not empty, if it is not, we create the SQL statement to search for products that match the search word, always with *$sql* variable. So *$sql* varia-ble takes a different value based on what we need to get from the database.

Then *$sql* is used by PHP function that executes the query: *mysq-li_query()*, line 36. This is an example of dynamically using a va-riable based on our needs. The result will be the same, i.e. a list of products, but the products displayed will be different.

Here is the SQL statement used for the query based on the visi-tor's search term:

$sql="**select * from PHP_course_products where product_name LIKE '% $ search%' order by product_name**";

The new element in this statement is inside the **where** clause. This searches for the *occurrence* of the string within the table field, using the **LIKE** statement. This way we get a *broader* sear-ch. If a visitor types, for example, "*tec*", the products' name con-taining the string "*tec*" will be displayed: "*technics*", "*audiotecni-*

ca", "*visiotech*" (provided that we have products with that name in database).

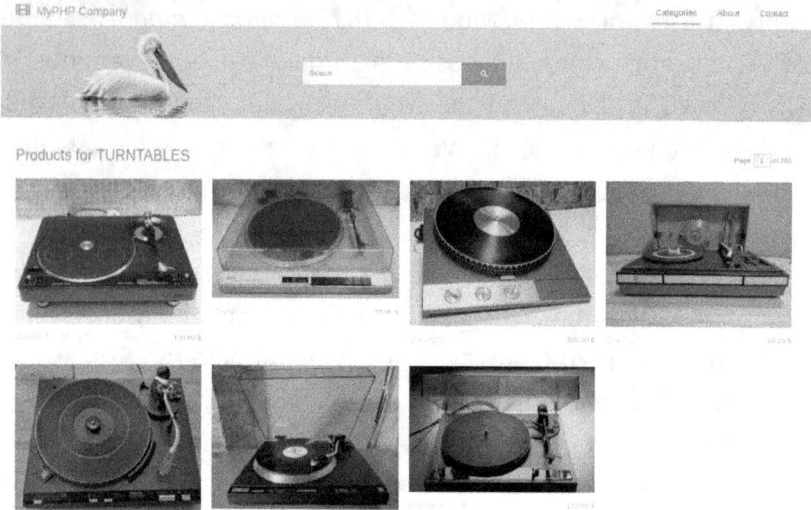

Products.php page showing products from the "*Turntables*" category.

By positioning on a product, its name and the link to detail page will appear.

<!=== Andrea Mauro Raimondi ===>

The last feature we had with the old graphics is the product detail page. Also in this case, it is a question of adapting the existing HTML code, adding PHP code to interact with our database.

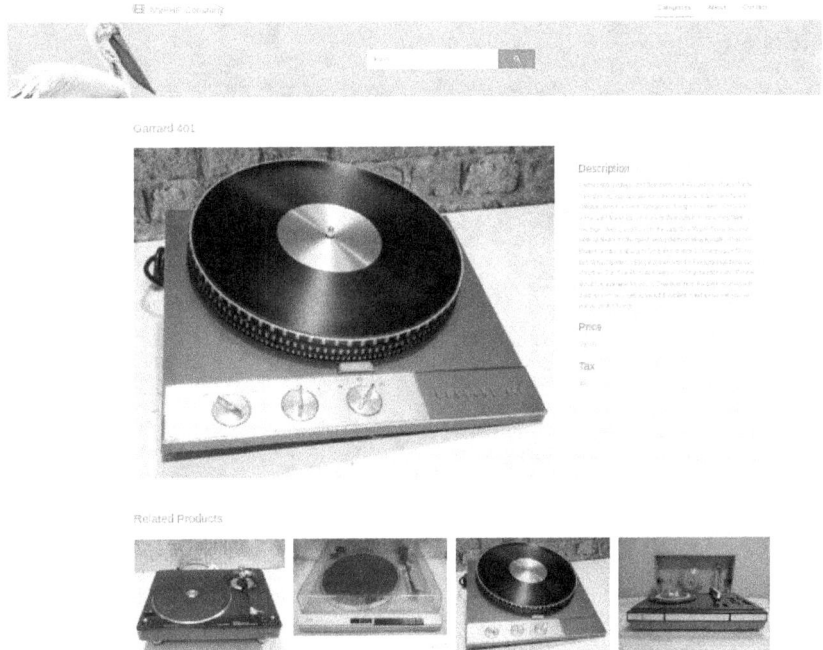

Here is the new product's detail page. In addition to product image, which now plays a central role, the other database's fields are displayed on the right.

We have also added a list of **related products,** while maintaining the chosen template setting. They are other products in the same category as the main product. Let's move on to PHP code of this page, *products_det.php.*

```php
1    <?php
2    include("zz_top.php");
3
4    $idprod = $_REQUEST["idprod"];
5
6    $sql = "select * from PHP_course_products where idproduct='$idprod' ";
7    $result = mysqli_query($connection,$sql) or die (mysqli_error());
8    $ValoriRiga = mysqli_fetch_array($result);
9    $idproduct = $ValoriRiga["idproduct"];
10   $idcategory = $ValoriRiga["idcategory"];
11   $product_name = $ValoriRiga["product_name"];
12   $description = $ValoriRiga["description"];
13   $quantity = $ValoriRiga["quantity"];
14   $price = $ValoriRiga["price"];
15   $tax = $ValoriRiga["tax"];
16 | $img = $ValoriRiga["img"];
17
18   ?>
19
20       <div class="container-fluid tm-container-content tm-mt-60">
21           <div class="row mb-4">
22               <h2 class="col-12 tm-text-primary"><?php print "$product_name";?></h2>
23           </div>
24           <div class="row tm-mb-90">
25               <div class="col-xl-8 col-lg-7 col-md-6 col-sm-12">
26                   <img src="../../img/<?php print "$img";?>" alt="Image" class="img-fluid">
27               </div>
28               <div class="col-xl-4 col-lg-5 col-md-6 col-sm-12">
29                   <div class="tm-bg-gray tm-video-details">
30
31                       <div class="mb-4">
32                           <h3 class="tm-text-gray-dark mb-3">Description</h3>
33                           <p><?php print "$description";?></p>
34                       </div>
35
36                       <div class="mb-4">
37                           <h3 class="tm-text-gray-dark mb-3">Price</h3>
38                           <p><?php print "$price";?></p>
39                       </div>
40
41                       <div class="mb-4">
42                           <h3 class="tm-text-gray-dark mb-3">Tax</h3>
43                           <p><?php print "$tax%";?></p>
44                       </div>
45
46                   </div>
47               </div>
48           </div>
49           <div class="row mb-4">
50               <h2 class="col-12 tm-text-primary">
51                   Related Products
52               </h2>
53           </div>
54           <div class="row mb-3 tm-gallery">
55   <?php
56   $sql = "select * from PHP_course_products where idcategory='$idcategory' order by product_name";
57   $result = mysqli_query($connection,$sql) or die (mysqli_error());
58   $tot = mysqli_num_rows($result);
59   while ($ValoriRiga = mysqli_fetch_array($result)) {
60   $idproduct = $ValoriRiga["idproduct"];
61   $idcategory = $ValoriRiga["idcategory"];
62   $product_name = $ValoriRiga["product_name"];
63   $description = $ValoriRiga["description"];
64   $quantity = $ValoriRiga["quantity"];
65   $price = $ValoriRiga["price"];
```

<!=== **Andrea Mauro Raimondi** ===>

```
56   $sql = "select * from PHP_course_products where idcategory='$idcategory' order by product_name";
57   $result = mysqli_query($connection,$sql) or die (mysqli_error());
58   $tot = mysqli_num_rows($result);
59   while ($ValoriRiga = mysqli_fetch_array($result)) {
60      $idproduct = $ValoriRiga["idproduct"];
61      $idcategory = $ValoriRiga["idcategory"];
62      $product_name = $ValoriRiga["product_name"];
63      $description = $ValoriRiga["description"];
64      $quantity = $ValoriRiga["quantity"];
65      $price = $ValoriRiga["price"];
66      $tax = $ValoriRiga["tax"];
67      $img = $ValoriRiga["img"];
68      ?>
69
70   <div class="col-xl-3 col-lg-4 col-md-6 col-sm-6 col-12 mb-5">
71         <figure class="effect-ming tm-video-item">
72            <img src="../../img/<?php print "$img";?>" alt="Image" class="img-fluid">
73            <figcaption class="d-flex align-items-center justify-content-center">
74               <h2><?php print "$product_name";?></h2>
75               <a href="products_det.php?idprod=<?php print "$idproduct";?>">Details</a>
76            </figcaption>
77         </figure>
78         <div class="d-flex justify-content-between tm-text-gray">
79            <span class="tm-text-gray-light">Quantity: <?php print "$quantity";?> </span>
80            <span><?php print "$price";?> $</span>
81         </div>
82      </div>
83   <?php
84   }
85   ?>
86      </div> <!-- row -->
87   </div> <!-- container-fluid, tm-container-content -->
88   <?php
89   include("zz_footer.php");
```

This page essentially retrieves the data relating to the product requested by the query string of the previous page, based on the visitor's click, lines 6-48. It shows also the products of the same category as the main product, as **related products**, lines 49-87. In line 4, the *$idprod* variable was retrieved from the query string.

We have seen how to replace an HTML graphics and reusing the PHP code used for a previous version of an application's public side. In the next few pages, we will discuss the changes taken place in back office area.

<?php Building Real World PHP Applications ?>

<!=== Andrea Mauro Raimondi ===>

BACK OFFICE AREA UPDATE

For the back office area, we looking for a template suitable for our purposes. Among those available we preferred Admin LTE3:

This template provides many HTML pages, CSS classes and java-script codes that make our application closer to the current taste. Below we compare old and new back office areas, or rather, the same back office with different graphics.

<?php Building Real World PHP Applications ?>

Before.

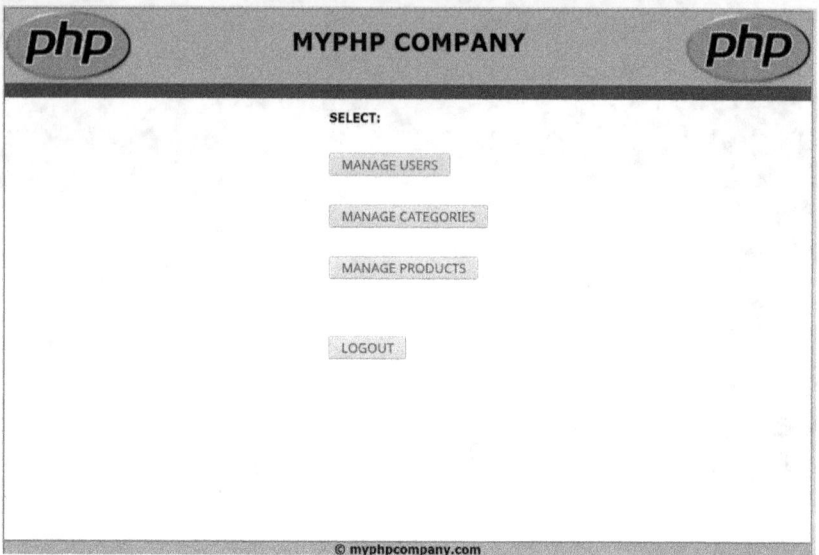

After

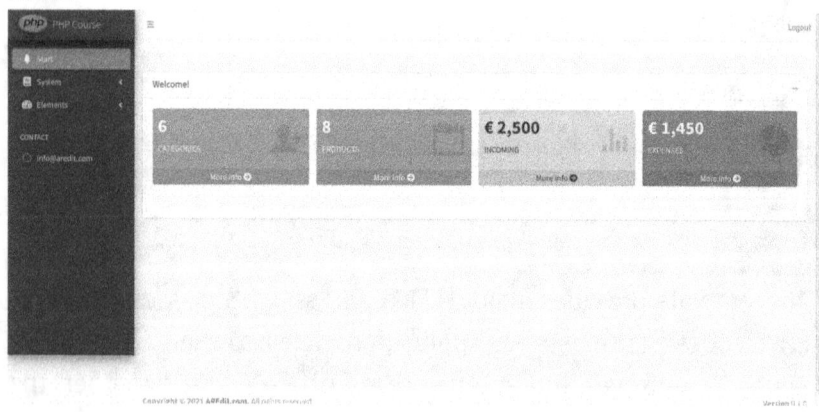

<!=== Andrea Mauro Raimondi ===>

In the new interface, we find a menu on the left with links to the various PHP pages, and the main area where the data is displayed and managed. In general, as for the public website, it is a matter of making the HTML pages dynamic by inserting the PHP code.

Since the template's part that changes is the central part, we can find the code that is repeated on each page and create separate files, which will be included in the main pages. Procedure is always the same: we create a PHP file for the *header*, which in this case contains the left column with the menu and a PHP file for the *footer*.

Surely template's HTML code is more complex than the previous one and you need to be careful where you put your hands, expecially if you are a beginner. In any case, by first understanding which template's area you are working on, even a beginner can use them and get excellent results.

We start deleting the HTML code that does not serve our purposes: such as repeated rows that simulate the data of a table or a set of rows, which will be replaced by records taken from our database.

In the chosen template some HTML pages are show the various elements of a form or examples of table formatting or other HTML elements that may be useful. It is a matter of copying the element's HTML code and inserting it into our pages.

Below is an example of AdminLTE3 page that shows the possible formatting for form fields:

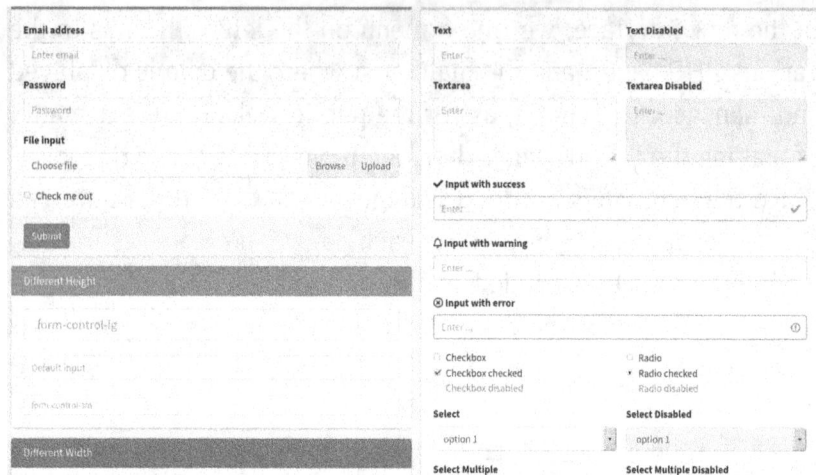

As we said, templates are heavily based on CSS use, as can be seen from the header code:

```
<!DOCTYPE html>
<html>
<head>
  <meta charset="utf-8">
  <meta http-equiv="X-UA-Compatible" content="IE=edge">
  <title>PHP Course !! Aredit.com</title>
  <!-- Tell the browser to be responsive to screen width -->
  <meta name="viewport" content="width=device-width, initial-scale=1">
  <!-- Font Awesome -->
  <link rel="stylesheet" href="./AdminLTE-3.0.4/plugins/fontawesome-free/css/all.min.css">
  <!-- Ionicons -->
  <link rel="stylesheet" href="https://code.ionicframework.com/ionicons/2.0.1/css/ionicons.min.css">
  <!-- Theme style -->
  <link rel="stylesheet" href="./AdminLTE-3.0.4/dist/css/adminlte.min.css">
  <!-- Google Font: Source Sans Pro -->
  <link href="https://fonts.googleapis.com/css?family=Source+Sans+Pro:300,400,400i,700" rel="stylesheet">


  <link rel="stylesheet" href="./AdminLTE-3.0.4/plugins/jquery-ui/jquery-ui.css">

  <link rel="stylesheet" href="./AdminLTE-3.0.4/plugins/select2/css/select2.min.css">

  <!-- fullCalendar -->
  <link rel="stylesheet" href="./AdminLTE-3.0.4/plugins/fullcalendar/main.min.css">
  <link rel="stylesheet" href="./AdminLTE-3.0.4/plugins/fullcalendar-daygrid/main.min.css">
  <link rel="stylesheet" href="./AdminLTE-3.0.4/plugins/fullcalendar-timegrid/main.min.css">
  <link rel="stylesheet" href="./AdminLTE-3.0.4/plugins/fullcalendar-bootstrap/main.min.css">
  <!-- DataTables -->
  <link rel="stylesheet" href="./AdminLTE-3.0.4/plugins/datatables-bs4/css/dataTables.bootstrap4.min.css">
  <link rel="stylesheet" href="./AdminLTE-3.0.4/plugins/datatables-responsive/css/responsive.bootstrap4.min.css">

  <!-- Bootstrap Color Picker -->
  <link rel="stylesheet" href="./AdminLTE-3.0.4/plugins/bootstrap-colorpicker/css/bootstrap-colorpicker.min.css">
```

<!=== Andrea Mauro Raimondi ===>

This is the back office new login form:

This page URL:
https://www.aredit.com/public/phpcourse/catalog/new/admin/login.php

<?php Building Real World PHP Applications ?>

```
132    ?>|
133  ▼ <div class="login-box">
134  ▼   <div class="login-logo">
135        <a href="login.php"><b>PHP Course<br>Catalog WebAPP</b></a>
136      </div>
137      <!-- /.login-logo -->
138  ▼   <div class="card">
139  ▼     <div class="card-body login-card-body">
140          <p class="login-box-msg"><?php print "LOGIN";?></p>
141
142          <form action="login.php" method="post">
143          <input type="hidden" name="lang" value="<?php print "";?>">
144  ▼        <div class="input-group mb-3">
145             <input type="text" class="form-control" name="userk" placeholder="Email" value="<?php print "$userk";?>">
146  ▼          <div class="input-group-append">
147  ▼            <div class="input-group-text">
148                 <span class="fas fa-envelope"></span>
149               </div>
150             </div>
151           </div>
152  ▼        <div class="input-group mb-3">
153             <input type="password" name="passk" class="form-control" placeholder="Password">
154  ▼          <div class="input-group-append">
155  ▼            <div class="input-group-text">
156                 <span class="fas fa-lock"></span>
157               </div>
158             </div>
159           </div>
160  ▼        <div class="row">
161  ▼          <div class="col-8">
162             </div>
163             <!-- /.col -->
164  ▼          <div class="col-4">
165               <button type="submit" class="btn btn-primary btn-block"><?php print "ENTER";?></button>
166             </div>
167             <!-- /.col -->
168           </div>
169          </form>
170
171          <p class="mb-1">
172            <a href="forgot-password.php?lang=<?php print "$lang";?>"><?php print "Forgot Password";?>?></a>
173          </p>
174          <p class="mb-0">
175            <a href="register.php" class="text-center"><?php print "";?></a>
176          </p>
177        </div>
178        <!-- /.login-card-body -->
179      </div>
180    </div>
```

This is the login page HTML code, as you can see, the <div></div> tags combined with CSS classes are used a lot.

<!=== Andrea Mauro Raimondi ===>

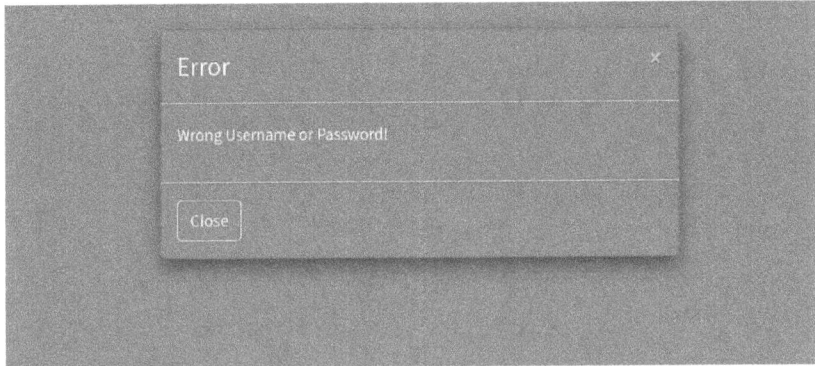

This is the new error message: it is a modal window, obtained using JQuery, lines 53-57.

```php
46    $passk=trim($passk);
47    $sqlb = "SELECT * FROM PHP course users WHERE username='$userk' AND password='$passk' and active='1'";
48    $resultb = mysqli_query($connection,$sqlb) or die(mysqli_error($connection));
49    $esiste=mysqli_num_rows($resultb);
50    if($esiste<= 0) {
51    ?>
52    <!-- jQuery -->
53    <script src="./AdminLTE-3.0.4/plugins/jquery/jquery.min.js"></script>
54    <!-- Bootstrap 4 -->
55    <script src="./AdminLTE-3.0.4/plugins/bootstrap/js/bootstrap.bundle.min.js"></script>
56    <!-- AdminLTE App -->
57    <script src="./AdminLTE-3.0.4/dist/js/adminlte.min.js"></script>
58        <div class="modal fade" id="modal-danger">
59            <div class="modal-dialog">
60                <div class="modal-content bg-danger">
61                    <div class="modal-header">
62                        <h4 class="modal-title">Error</h4>
63                        <button type="button" class="close" data-dismiss="modal" aria-label="Close">
64                            <span aria-hidden="true">&times;</span>
65                        </button>
66                    </div>
67                    <div class="modal-body">
68                        <p><?php print "Wrong Username or Password";?>!</p>
69                    </div>
70                    <div class="modal-footer justify-content-between">
71                        <button type="button" class="btn btn-outline-light" data-dismiss="modal">Close</button>
72                    </div>
73                </div>
74                <!-- /.modal-content -->
75            </div>
76            <!-- /.modal-dialog -->
77        </div>
78        <!-- /.modal -->
79    <script>
80    $('#modal-danger').modal('show');
81    $('#modal-danger').on('hidden.bs.modal', function (e) {
82        document.location.href="login.php?lang=<?php print "";?>";
83    })
84    </script>
85    <?php
86    exit;
87    }
```

The error message appears if the record corresponding to the username and password entered at login is not found.

Pages' logic and the PHP code remain essentially the same as previously used.

To better understand new graphics possibilities, after checking the correctness of the login data, the user is directed to a new page, called *start.php*, line 113, which represents a sort of *dashboard*. In it, we may highlight some application parameters available: the number of categories, the number of products, and hypothetical sales data.

```
104    $sql2 = "Insert Into PHP_course_logutenti_admin (IDUSER,SESSIONID,STATE,CREATIONDATE,IP,URL) ";
105    $sql2 = $sql2." values ('$iduser','$mysessionid','1','Soggi','$REMOTE_ADDR','')";
106    $result2 = mysqli_query($connection,$sql2) or die(mysqli_error($connection));
107
108    $sql_up = "update PHP_course_users set naccess=naccess+1 where iduser='$iduser'";
109    $result_up = mysqli_query($connection,$sql_up) or die(mysqli_error($connection));
110
111    ?>
112  ▼ <script>
113        document.location.href="start.php?mysessionid=<?php print "$mysessionid";?>&idu=<?php print "$iduser";?>";
114    </script>
115    <?php
116    }
117    }
```

"Dashboard" of the *start.php* page:

The following code shows the database calls that retrieve the total number of categories and products, lines 47-54, these data are then inserted in the HTML code of the template's original dashboard, after eliminating the undesired code.

Questa la dashboard del template

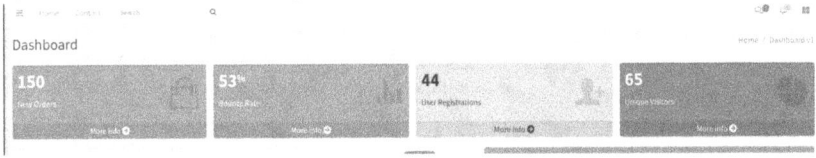

<?php Building Real World PHP Applications ?>

```php
45
46  <?php
47  $sql = "select * from PHP_course_categories";
48  $result = mysqli_query($connection,$sql) or die (mysqli_error($connection));
49  $total_categories = mysqli_num_rows($result);
50
51
52  $sql = "select * from PHP_course_products";
53  $result = mysqli_query($connection,$sql) or die (mysqli_error($connection));
54  $total_products = mysqli_num_rows($result);
55  ?>
56
57              <div class="row">
58                  <div class="col-lg-3 col-6">
59                      <!-- small box -->
60                      <div class="small-box bg-info">
61                          <div class="inner">
62                              <h3> <?php print "$total_categories";?></h3>
63
64                              <p><?php print "CATEGORIES";?></p>
65                          </div>
66                          <div class="icon">
67                              <i class="ion ion-person-add"></i>
68                          </div>
69                          <a href="categories.php?<?php print "$strquerystr";?>" class="small-box-footer"
70                          right"></i></a>
71                      </div>
72                  </div>
73                  <!-- ./col -->
74                  <div class="col-lg-3 col-6">
75                      <!-- small box -->
76                      <div class="small-box bg-success">
77                          <div class="inner">
78                              <h3> <?php print "$total_products";?></h3>
79                              <p><?php print "PRODUCTS";?></p>
80                          </div>
81                          <div class="icon">
82                              <i class="ion ion-calendar"></i>
83                          </div>
84                          <a href="products.php?<?php print "$strquerystr";?>" class="small-box-footer">M
                           right"></i></a>
```

<!=== Andrea Mauro Raimondi ===>

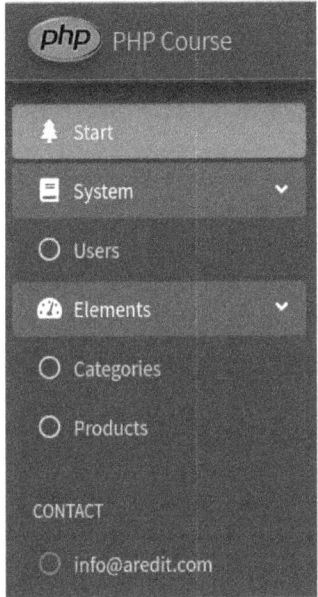

From the side menu, it is possible to access the various management pages: user, category, and product management.

The menu items, thanks to the CSS and JQuery features, are grouped. Submenu items are displayed if you select the relative group name, such as "*System*", which contains the user management, or "*Elements*" which contains categories and products management.

<?php Building Real World PHP Applications ?>

Below the new category management page.

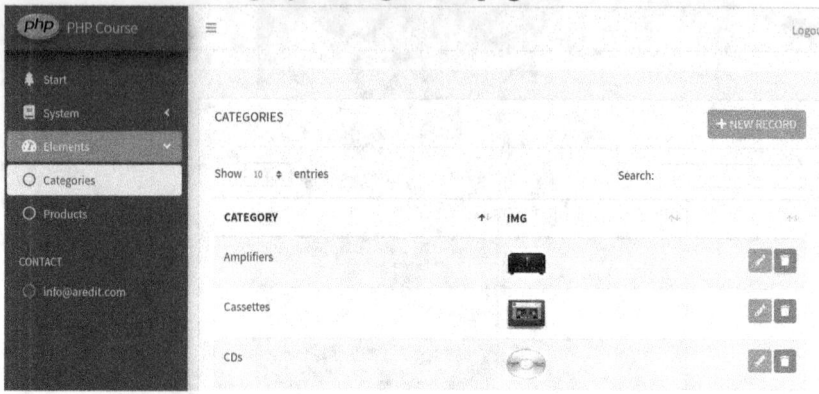

Here is thed new form for add or modify categories data:

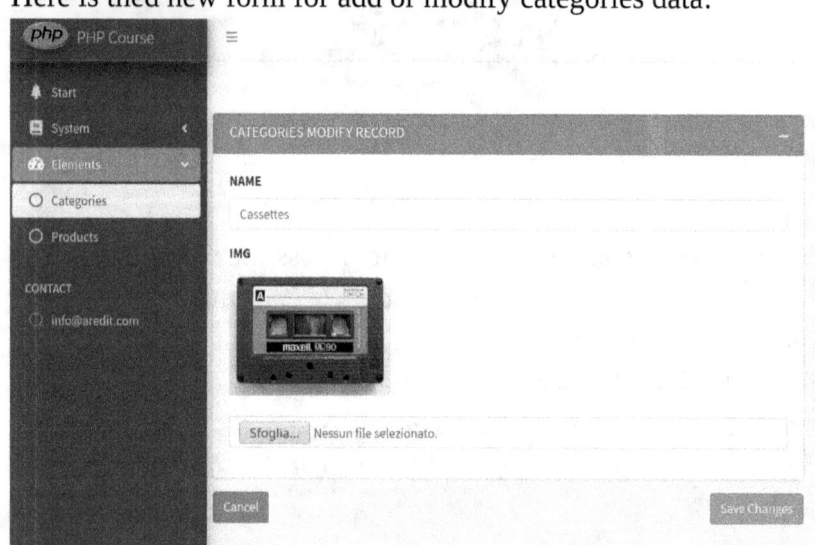

The warning message before deleting a record:

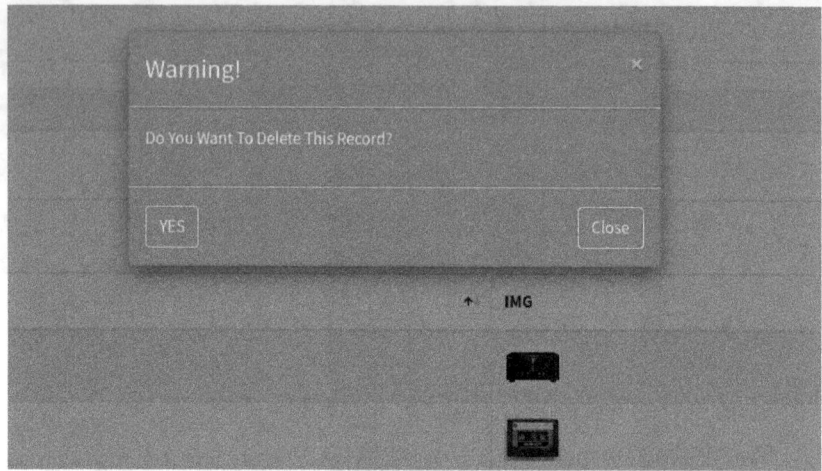

Also for this version, the behavior of the category management

```
12 ▼ if(isset($action)){
13
14 ▼      if ($action == "add") {
15              $msg = "ADD NEW RECORD";
16              $d=date("d/m/Y");
17              $idcategory=0;
18              writeform() ;
19              exit;
20          }
21
22 ▼      if ($action == "mod") {
23              $msg = "MODIFY RECORD";
24              $sqlb = "SELECT * FROM PHP_course_categories WHERE idcategory='$idcategory'";
25              $resultb = mysqli_query($connection,$sqlb) or die(mysqli_error());
26 ▼          while ($ValoriRigab = mysqli_fetch_array($resultb)) {
27                  $idcategory = $ValoriRigab["idcategory"];
28                  $category = $ValoriRigab["category"];
29                  $img = $ValoriRigab["img"];
30              }
31              $action2 = "mod";
32              writeform() ;
33              exit;
34          }
35
36 ▼      if ($action == "delete") {
37          $sql = "DELETE FROM PHP_course_categories WHERE idcategory='$idcategory'";
38          $result = mysqli_query($connection,$sql);
39          if (! $result)
40 ▼        {
41          echo "<b>ERROR!</b>";
42          }
43          else
44 ▼        {
45          echo "RECORD DELETED.";
46          ?>
```

page varies according to the value of the variable *$action*, as seen on line 14.

The same for the product management page.

The new graphics allow a good page display even on devices other than PC monitors: below you can see the same page on a smaller screen.

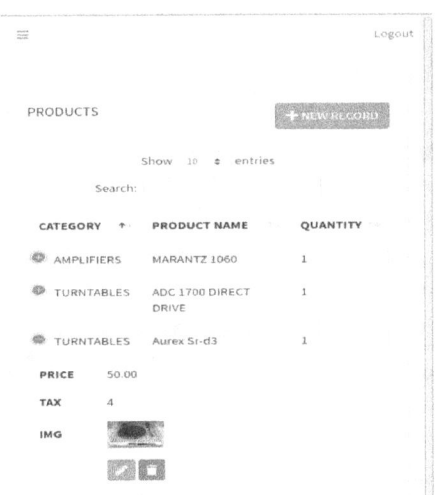

Table size is automatically changed based on the width of the screen. This happens through the settings of template's CSS files. Furthermore, this HTML table is based on JQuery code to provide advanced functions not only for viewing but also for searching data inside the same table, as can be seen from the "*Search*" field above table headers. We can avoid writing a lot of PHP code to achieve the same effect provided by the included javascript.

Below the new *products form*:

Appendix 1

PHP TUTORIAL

PHP is a **server-side scripting** language and a powerful tool for creating dynamic and interactive web pages.

PHP is the recursive acronym for "PHP: Hypertext Preprocessor".

PHP 7 is the latest stable version.

A PHP script is executed on the server and the HTML result is sent to the browser.

A PHP script can be placed anywhere in the document.

A PHP script starts with **<?php** and ends with **?>**:

```
<? php
// The PHP code goes here
?>
```

The default extension for PHP files is "**.php**".

A PHP file usually contains HTML tags and PHP scripting code.

PHP instructions end with a semicolon (**;**).

In PHP, keywords (e.g. if, else, while, echo, etc.), user-defined classes, functions, and functions are not case sensitive.

However, **all variable names are case-sensitive**!

<!=== Andrea Mauro Raimondi ===>

PHP Comments

A comment in the PHP code is a line that is not executed as part of the program. Its only purpose is to be read by someone who is looking at the code.

Comments can be used for:

Allow others to understand your code.

Remind yourself what you did - Most programmers have experienced going back to their jobs a year or two later and having to re-figure what they did. Comments can remind you of what you were thinking when you wrote the code.

PHP supports several type of comment:

Single line comment

```
<!DOCTYPE html>
<html>
<body>

<?php
// This is a single-line comment

# This is also a single-line comment
?>

</body>
</html>
```

Multiple lines:

```
<!DOCTYPE html>
<html>
<body>

<?php
/*
This is a multiple-lines comment block
that spans over multiple
lines
*/
?>

</body>
</html>
```

Or to exclude parts of the code:

```
<!DOCTYPE html>
<html>
<body>

<?php
// You can also use comments to leave out parts of a code line
$x = 5 /* + 15 */ + 5;
echo $x;
?>

</body>
</html>
```

<!=== Andrea Mauro Raimondi ===>

VARIABLES

Variables are "*containers*" for storing information.

In PHP, a variable begins with a $ sign, followed by the variable name:

```php
<?php
$txt = "I'm a string variable!";
$x = 71;
$y = 10.8;
?>
```

After the execution of previous instructions, the *$txt* variable will contain value *"I'm a string variable!"*, The *$x* variable will contain value *71* and the *$y* variable will contain value *10.8*.

Remember: when assigning a text value to a variable, put quotation marks around its value.

Unlike other programming languages, PHP has no command to *declare* a variable. It is created when you first assign a value to it.

A variable can have a short name (such as x and y) or a more descriptive name (age, catname, total_volume).

Rules for PHP variables:

A variable begins with a $ sign, followed by the variable name.

A variable name must begin with a letter or underscore.

A variable name cannot start with a number.

Variable names are *case-sensitive* ($**c**ar and $**C**ar are two different variables).

<?php Building Real World PHP Applications ?>

PHP variable scope

In PHP, variables can be *declared* anywhere in the script. The *scope* of a variable is the part of the script where the variable can be referenced/used.

PHP has three different variable scopes:

Local

Global

Static

A variable declared outside of a function has a GLOBAL PURPOSE and can only be accessed outside of a function:

```
1   <!DOCTYPE html>
2   <html>
3   <body>
4
5   <?php
6   $x = 5; // global scope
7
8   function myFunction() {
9       // using x inside this function will generate an error
10      echo "<p>Variable x inside function is: $x</p>";
11  } |
12  myFunction();
13
14  echo "<p>Variable x outside function is: $x</p>";
15  ?>
16
17  </body>
18  </html>
```

<!=== Andrea Mauro Raimondi ===>

```php
1  <?php
2  function myFunction() {
3    $x = 5; // local scope
4    echo "<p>Variable x inside function is: $x</p>";
5  }
6  myFunction();
7
8  // using x outside the function will generate an error
9  echo "<p>Variable x outside function is: $x</p>";
10  ?>
```

A variable declared *within* a function has a LOCAL SCOPE and can only be accessed within that function: It is possible to have local variables with the same name in different functions because local variables are only recognized by the function in which they are declared.

The *global* keyword is used to access a global variable from within a function.

```php
<?php
$x = 5;
$y = 10;

function myFunction() {
  global $x, $y; //<===========|
  $y = $x + $y;
}

myFunction();
echo $y; // outputs 15
?>
```

Usually, when a function is completed/executed, all its variables are deleted. However, sometimes we want a local variable NOT to be deleted. We need it for further work. To do this, we use the *static* keyword when declaring the variable for the first time. That way, every time the function is called, that variable will still have the information it contained from the last time the function was called.

```
<!DOCTYPE html>
<html>
<body>

<?php
function myFunction() {
  static $x = 10;
  echo "variable is $x";
  $x++;
}

myFunction();
echo "<br>";
myFunction();
echo "<br>";
myFunction();
?>

</body>
</html>
```

variable is 10
variable is 11
variable is 12

<!=== Andrea Mauro Raimondi ===>

In PHP, there are two basic ways to get the output, to print the information: *echo* and *print*.

echo and *print* are more or less the same thing. Both are used to send data to the screen.

The differences are minimal: *echo* has no return value while *print* has a return value of 1, so it can be used in expressions. *echo* can take multiple parameters (although such use is rare) while *print* can take one argument. *echo* is slightly faster than *print*.

The text to be displayed must be contained in quotation marks.

```
<!DOCTYPE html>
<html>
<body>

<?php
$txt1 = "Learn PHP";
$txt2 = "AREdit.com";
$x = 7;
$y = 0;

echo "echo:<br><h2>" . $txt1 . "</h2>";
echo "Study PHP at " . $txt2 . "<br>";
echo $x + $y;
echo "<hr><br>";
print "print:<br><h2>" . $txt1 . "</h2>";
print "Study PHP at " . $txt2 . "<br>";
print $x + $y;
?>

</body>
</html>
```

echo:

Learn PHP

Study PHP at AREdit.com
7

---

print:

Learn PHP

Study PHP at AREdit.com
7

<?php Building Real World PHP Applications ?>

Data Type

Variables can store data of different types, and different types of data can do different things.
PHP supports the following data types:
String
Integer
Float (floating-point numbers - also called double)
Boolean
Array
Object
NULL
Resource

A **string**, is a sequence of characters, such as "*Hello world!*". A string can be any text enclosed in quotation marks. Both single and double.

An **integer** data type is a non-decimal number between -2.147.483.648 and 2.147.483.647.

Rules for integers:

An integer must contain at least one digit

An integer must not have a decimal point

An integer can be positive or negative

Integers can be specified in decimal (base 10), hexadecimal (base 16), octal (base 8), or binary (base 2) notation

<!=== Andrea Mauro Raimondi ===>

A **float** (floating-point number) is a number with a decimal point or an exponential number: $ x = 10.08

A **boolean** represents two possible states: TRUE or FALSE: $ x = true;

An **array** stores multiple values in a single variable, as we saw with variables that contained the result of a query, a recordset.

Classes and **objects** are the two main aspects of object-oriented programming. A *class* is an object model and an *object* is an instance of a class. When individual objects are created, they inherit all properties and behaviors from the class, but each object will have different values for the properties. *An object is a set of PHP functions.*

Null is a special data type that can have only one value: *NULL.* A variable of data type NULL is a variable that has no value assigned. If a variable is created without a value, it is automatically assigned a NULL value.

Main String Function

Here are the most used PHP functions for string manipulation:

strlen(*string*) - Returns the length of a string

str_word_count(*string*) - Counts the words in a string

strpos(*string, find, start*) - Search for text within a string

str_replace(*find, replace, string, count*) - Replace text within a string

addlashes(*string*) Return a backslashed string in front of: apostrophe ('), double quote ("), backslash (\), NULL. Useful when saving data in databases.

explode(*separator, string, limit*) splits a string into an array based on a character used as a separator

htmlentities(*string*) converts characters to HTML entities

number_format(*number, decimals, decimalpoint, separator*) formats a number by grouping the thousands

strtolower(*string*) converts a string to lowercase

strtoupper(*string*) converts a string to uppercase

substr(*string, start, length*) returns part of a string

substr_replace(*string, replacement, start, length*) replaces part of a string with another string

trim(*string, charlist*) removes spaces and other default characters from both sides of a string

<!=== Andrea Mauro Raimondi ===>

PHP and numbers

PHP provides automatic data type conversion. So, if you assign an integer value to a variable, that variable's type will automatically be an integer. If you later assign a string to the same variable, the type will change to a string. This can sometimes lead to code management problems, especially if calculations need to be done. To find out what data type you are working with, the following functions are useful:

is_int(*var*) checks if a variable is of type integer
is_float(*var*) checks if a variable is of type float
is_nan(*var*) checks if a variable is not a number
is_numeric(*var*) checks whether a variable is a number

PHP has several **math functions** that allow you to perform math tasks on numbers. Here are the most used ones, based on my experience.

min(*num, num, num,...*) and **max(*num, num, num,...*)** can be used to find the lowest or highest value in an argument list or array
abs(*num*) returns the **absolute(*positive*)** value of a number
round(*num*) rounds a floating-point number to the nearest integer
rand(*min, max*) generates a random number between min and max

PHP OPERATORS

Operators are used to perform operations on variables and values.
PHP divides the operators into the following groups:
    Arithmetic operators
    Assignment operators
    Comparison operators
    Increment / Decrement Operators
    Logical operators
    String operators
    Matrix operators
    Conditional assignment operators

Arithmetic operators are used with numeric values to perform
common arithmetic operations, such as addition, subtraction,
multiplication, etc.

Operator	Name	Example	Result
+	Addition	$x + $y	Sum of $x and $y
-	Subtraction	$x - $y	Difference of $x and $y
*	Multiplication	$x * $y	Product of $x and $y
/	Division	$x / $y	Quotient of $x and $y
%	Modulus	$x % $y	Remainder of $x divided by $y
**	Exponentiation	$x ** $y	Result of raising $x to the $y'th power

<!=== Andrea Mauro Raimondi ===>

Assignment operators are used with numeric values to write a value to a variable.

The basic assignment operator in PHP is "=". It means that the left operand is set to the value of the right assignment expression.

Assignment	Same as...	Description
x = y	x = y	The left operand gets set to the value of the expression on the right
x += y	x = x + y	Addition
x -= y	x = x - y	Subtraction
x *= y	x = x * y	Multiplication
x /= y	x = x / y	Division
x %= y	x = x % y	Modulus

Increment operators are used to increment a variable's value..
Decrement operators are used to decrement a variable's value..

Operator	Name	Description
++$x	Pre-increment	Increments $x by one, then returns $x
$x++	Post-increment	Returns $x, then increments $x by one
--$x	Pre-decrement	Decrements $x by one, then returns $x
$x--	Post-decrement	Returns $x, then decrements $x by one

PHP **comparison operators** are used to compare two values (number or string).

Operator	Name	Example	Result
==	Equal	$x == $y	Returns true if $x is equal to $y
===	Identical	$x === $y	Returns true if $x is equal to $y, and they are of the same type
!=	Not equal	$x != $y	Returns true if $x is not equal to $y
<>	Not equal	$x <> $y	Returns true if $x is not equal to $y
!==	Not identical	$x !== $y	Returns true if $x is not equal to $y, or they are not of the same type
>	Greater than	$x > $y	Returns true if $x is greater than $y
<	Less than	$x < $y	Returns true if $x is less than $y
>=	Greater than or equal to	$x >= $y	Returns true if $x is greater than or equal to $y
<=	Less than or equal to	$x <= $y	Returns true if $x is less than or equal to $y
<=>	Spaceship	$x <=> $y	Returns an integer less than, equal to, or greater than zero, depending on if $x is less than, equal to, or greater than $y. Introduced in PHP 7.

PHP **logical operators** are used to combine conditional statements.

Operator	Name	Example	Result
and	And	$x and $y	True if both $x and $y are true
or	Or	$x or $y	True if either $x or $y is true
xor	Xor	$x xor $y	True if either $x or $y is true, but not both
&&	And	$x && $y	True if both $x and $y are true
||	Or	$x || $y	True if either $x or $y is true
!	Not	!$x	True if $x is not true

<!=== Andrea Mauro Raimondi ===>

PHP has two operators designed specifically for **strings**

Operator	Name	Example	Result
.	Concatenation	$txt1 . $txt2	Concatenation of $txt1 and $txt2
.=	Concatenation assignment	$txt1 .= $txt2	Appends $txt2 to $txt1

Array operators are used to compare arrays

Operator	Name	Example	Result
+	Union	$x + $y	Union of $x and $y
==	Equality	$x == $y	Returns true if $x and $y have the same key/value pairs
===	Identity	$x === $y	Returns true if $x and $y have the same key/value pairs in the same order and of the same types
!=	Inequality	$x != $y	Returns true if $x is not equal to $y
<>	Inequality	$x <> $y	Returns true if $x is not equal to $y
!==	Non-identity	$x !== $y	Returns true if $x is not identical to $y

<?php Building Real World PHP Applications ?>

PHP **conditional assignment operators** are used to set a value depending on conditions

Operator	Name	Example	Result
?:	Ternary	$x = expr1 ? expr2 : expr3	Returns the value of $x. The value of $x is expr2 if expr1 = TRUE. The value of $x is expr3 if expr1 = FALSE
??	Null coalescing	$x = expr1 ?? expr2	Returns the value of $x. The value of $x is expr1 if expr1 exists, and is not NULL. If expr1 does not exist, or is NULL, the value of $x is expr2. Introduced in PHP 7

<!=== Andrea Mauro Raimondi ===>

PHP Conditional Statements

Conditional statements are used to perform different actions based on different conditions.
In PHP we have the following conditional statements:
   if statement - executes code if a condition is true
   if ... else statement - executes some code if a condition is true and another code if that condition is false
   if ... elseif ... else statement - executes different code for more than two conditions
   switch statement: selects one of the many possible blocks of code to execute
Example of *if ... else*

```
<!DOCTYPE html>
<html>
<body>

<?php
$t = date("H");

if ($t < "20") {
  echo "Have a good day!";
} else {
  echo "Have a good night!";
}
?>

</body>
</html>
```

Have a good day!

if...elseif...else example:

```
<!DOCTYPE html>
<html>
<body>
<?php
$t = date("H");
echo "<p>The hour (of the server) is " . $t;
echo ", and will give the following message:</p>";

if ($t < "10") {
  echo "Have a good morning!";
} elseif ($t < "20") {
  echo "Have a good day!";
} else {
  echo "Have a good night!";
}
?>
</body>
</html>
```

The hour (of the server) is 10, and will give the following message:
Have a good day!

switch example:

```
<!DOCTYPE html>
<html>
<body>
<?php
$favcolor = "blue";
$mytext = "Your favorite color is";
print "$mytext";
switch ($favcolor) {
  case "red":
    echo " red!";
    break;
  case "blue":
    echo " blue!";
    break;
  case "green":
    echo "green!";
    break;
  default:
    echo " neither red, blue, nor green!";
}
?>
```

Your favorite color is blue!

Switch works like this: first, we have a single *n expression* (most often a variable), like *$favcolor* in this example, which is evaluated once. The value of the expression is then compared to the values for *each case* in the structure. If there is a match, the code

<!=== Andrea Mauro Raimondi ===>

block associated with that *case* is executed. You need to insert the *break* statement to prevent the code from automatically executing in the next *case*. The *default* statement is used if no match is found in other *cases*.

<?php Building Real World PHP Applications ?>

PHP LOOPS

Loops are used to execute the same block of code multiple times as long as a certain condition is true.

In PHP, we have the following types of loops:

while - iterates a block of code until the specified condition is true

do ... while - iterates a block of code once, then repeats the loop until the specified condition is true

for - repeats a block of code a specified number of times

foreach - Executes a block of code for each element in an array

The while loop executes a block of code as long as the specified condition is true.

```
<!DOCTYPE html>
<html>
<body>

<?php
$x = 0;

while($x <= 100) {
  echo "The number is: $x <br>";
  $x+=10;
}
?>

</body>
</html>
```

The number is: 0
The number is: 10
The number is: 20
The number is: 30
The number is: 40
The number is: 50
The number is: 60
The number is: 70
The number is: 80
The number is: 90
The number is: 100

<!=== Andrea Mauro Raimondi ===>

The **do ... while** loop always executes the block of code once, then checks the condition and repeats the loop until the specified condition is true.

The following example first sets a *$x* variable to 1 ($x = 1). Then, the *do while loop* will write an output and then increment the variable *$x* by 1. Then the condition is checked (*is $x less than or equal to 5?*) And the loop will continue to execute as long as *$x* is less than or equal to 5:

```
<!DOCTYPE html>
<html>
<body>
<?php
$x = 1;
do {
    echo "The number is: $x <br>";
    $x++;
} while ($x <= 5);
?>
</body>
</html>
```

The number is: 1
The number is: 2
The number is: 3
The number is: 4
The number is: 5

Warning: in a *do ... while loop*, the condition is checked AFTER executing the statements inside the loop. This means that the *do ... while* loop will execute its statements at least once, even if the condition is false.

The **for** loop is used when you know in advance how many times the script should run.

for(*init counter; test counter; increment counter*) {
   code to execute for each iteration;
}

Parameters:

    init counter: initializes the value of the loop counter

    test counter: evaluated for each iteration of the loop. If it returns TRUE, the loop continues. If it returns FALSE, the loop ends.

    increment counter: increases the value of the loop counter

```
<!DOCTYPE html>
<html>
<body>

<?php
for ($x = 0; $x <= 10; $x++) {
  echo "The number is: $x <br>";
}
?>

</body>
</html>
```

The number is: 0
The number is: 1
The number is: 2
The number is: 3
The number is: 4
The number is: 5
The number is: 6
The number is: 7
The number is: 8
The number is: 9
The number is: 10

$x = 0; - Initialize the loop counter ($x) and set the initial value to 0
$x<= 10; - Continue the loop until $x is less than or equal to 10
$x++ - Increases the loop counter value by 1 for each iteration

<!=== Andrea Mauro Raimondi ===>

The **foreach** loop works only on *arrays* and is used to iterate each key/value pair in an array.

foreach($array as $value) {
  code to execute;
}

```
<!DOCTYPE html>
<html>
<body>

<?php
$cars = array("BMW", "Mercedes", "Fiat", "Ford");

foreach ($cars as $value) {
  echo "$value <br>";
}
?>

</body>
</html>
```

BMW
Mercedes
Fiat
Ford

For each loop iteration, the value of the current array element is assigned to *$value* and the *array pointer* is shifted by one, until it reaches the last element.

We previously mentioned the **break** statement in **while** loops that interrupt the execution of a block of code. The **continue** statement breaks one iteration (in the loop), if a specified condition occurs, and continues with the next iteration in the loop.

This example skips the value 5:

```
<!DOCTYPE html>
<html>
<body>

<?php
for ($x = 0; $x < 15; $x++) {
  if ($x == 5) {
    continue;
  }
  echo "The number is: $x <br>";
}
?>

</body>
</html>
```

The number is: 0
The number is: 1
The number is: 2
The number is: 3
The number is: 4
The number is: 6
The number is: 7
The number is: 8
The number is: 9
The number is: 10
The number is: 11
The number is: 12
The number is: 13
The number is: 14

<!=== Andrea Mauro Raimondi ===>

PHP Functions

In addition to the built-in PHP functions, you can create your functions. A *function* is a block of instructions that can be used repeatedly in a program. A function will not be executed automatically when a page is loaded.

A function will be executed by a **call** to the function.

A user-defined function declaration begins with the word function:

function *functionName*() **{**
  code to execute;
}

Warning: A *function name* must start with a letter or underscore. Function names are NOT case sensitive.

Hint: Give the function a name that reflects what the function does!

```
<!DOCTYPE html>
<html>
<body>
<?php
function write_txt() {
  echo "Today is a wonderful
day!";
}

write_txt();
?>
</body>
</html>
```

Today is a wonderful day!

<?php Building Real World PHP Applications ?>

In the previous example, we create a function named "*write_txt()*". The *opening brace* ({) indicates the start of the function code and the *closing brace* (}) indicates the end of the function. The function writes "*Today is a wonderful day!*".

To *call* the function, just write its name followed by brackets ():
write_txt();

Information can be passed to functions via *arguments*. An argument is just like a variable.

The arguments are specified after the function name, inside the parentheses. You can add as many arguments as you like, separated with a comma.

The following example presents a function with *two arguments* (*$fname* and *$year*). When the *familyName()* function is called, we also pass a name and a year (e.g. *Filippo, 2010*), and the name and year are used within the function, which returns different first names and years, but the same family name:

```
<!DOCTYPE html>
<html>
<body>

<?php
function familyName($fname, $year) {
  echo "$fname Raimondi. Born in $year
<br>";
}

familyName("Filippo","2010");
familyName("Andrea","1971");
familyName("Massimiliano","2012");
?>
```

Filippo Raimondi. Born in 2010
Andrea Raimondi. Born in 1971
Massimiliano Raimondi. Born in 2012

<!=== Andrea Mauro Raimondi ===>

The following example shows how to use a default parameter. If we call the *setSize()* function with no arguments, it takes the *default* value as an argument:

```
<!DOCTYPE html>
<html>
<body>

<?php
function setSize(int $size = 50) {
  echo "The size is : $size cm.<br>";
}

setSize(350);
setSize();
setSize(135);
setSize(80);
?>

</body>
</html>
```

```
The size is : 350 cm.
The size is : 50 cm.
The size is : 135 cm.
The size is : 80 cm.
```

A function can return a value, using the **return** statement:

```
<!DOCTYPE html>
<html>
<body>
<?php
function sum(int $x, int $y) {
  $z = $x + $y;
  return $z;
}
echo "5 + 10 = " . sum(5,10) . "<br>";
echo "7 + 13 = " . sum(7,13) . "<br>";
echo "2 + 4 = " . sum(2,4);
?>
</body>
</html>
```

```
5 + 10 = 15
7 + 13 = 20
2 + 4 = 6
```

ARRAY

An array is a special variable, which can hold more than one value at a time. If you have a list of items (a list of city names, for example), storing cities in individual variables might look like this:

```
$cars1 = "Milan";
$cars2 = "New York";
$cars3 = "Tokyo";
```

However, what if you want to scroll through the cities and find a specific one? What if we don't have 3 cities, but 300?

The solution is to create an array!

An array can contain many values under one name, and the values can be accessed by referencing a numeric index:

```
<? php
$cities = array("Milan", "New York", "Tokyo");
echo "I like". $cities [0]. ",". $cities [1]. "and". $cities [2]. ".";
?>
```

The *array()* function is used to create an array, as seen in the example above. In PHP, there are *three types of arrays*:

Indexed Arrays: Arrays with a numeric index

Associative Arrays: Arrays with named keys

Multidimensional Arrays: Arrays containing one or more arrays

<!=== Andrea Mauro Raimondi ===>

There are two ways to create indexed arrays:
The index can be assigned automatically (***index always starts at 0***), like this:
$cars = array("Volvo", "BMW", "Toyota");
or the index can be assigned manually:
$cars [0] = "Volvo";
$cars [1] = "BMW";
$cars [2] = "Toyota";
To loop and print all the values of an indexed array, we usually use a *for loop*, like this:

```
<!DOCTYPE html>
<html>
<body>
<?php
$cars = array("Volvo", "BMW", "Toyota");
$arrlength = count($cars);

for($x = 0; $x < $arrlength; $x++) {
  echo $x.")".$cars[$x];
  echo "<hr>";
}
?>
</body>
</html>
```

0)Volvo
_____

1)BMW
_____

2)Toyota
_____

Associative arrays are arrays that use nominal keys.

There are two ways to create an associative array:

$birthplace = array("Massy" => "Milan", "Marta" => "Dever", "Silvia" => "Paris");

or:

$birthplace ["Massy"] = "Milan";

$birthplace ["Martha"] = "Dever";

$birthplace ["Silvia"] = "Paris";

To loop and print all the values of an associative array, you can use a *foreach loop*, like this:

```
<!DOCTYPE html>
<html>
<body>

<?php
$birthplace = array ("Massy" => "Milano",
"Marta" => "Dever", "Silvia" => "Paris");

foreach($birthplace as $x => $x_value) {
  echo "Key=" . $x . ", Value=" . $x_value;
  echo "<br>";
}
?>

</body>
</html>
```

```
Key=Massy, Value=Milano
Key=Marta, Value=Dever
Key=Silvia, Value=Paris
```

The array types seen so far consist of a single list of key/value pairs. Sometimes you want to store values with more than one key. For this, there are **multidimensional arrays**.

A multidimensional array is an array containing one or more arrays. PHP supports multidimensional arrays with depths of two, three, four, five, or more levels. In any case, arrays with a depth greater than three levels are difficult to manage and little used.

{200}

<!=== Andrea Mauro Raimondi ===>

The size of an array indicates the number of indices needed to select an element. For a *two-dimensional array*, two indices are required to select an element. For a *three-dimensional array*, three indices are required to select an element. A two-dimensional array is an array of arrays (a three-dimensional array is an array of arrays of arrays).

Let's see an example of a *two-dimensional array*, starting from the following table:

Name	Weight	Height
Filippo	70	1.80
Andrea	65	1.70
Silvia	45	1.75
Marta	48	1.78

We can store the data from the table in a two-dimensional array, like this:

```
$names = array (
  array ("Filippo", 70,1.80),
  array ("Andrea", 65,1.70),
  array ("Silvia", 45,1.75),
  array ("Marta", 48,1.78)
);
```

Now the two-dimensional array *$names* contains four arrays and has two indexes: row and column.

To access the elements of the *$names* array we must point to the two indexes (row and column):

```php
<?php
$names = array (
  array ("Filippo", 70,1.80),
  array ("Andrea", 65,1.70),
  array ("Silvia", 45,1.75),
  array ("Marta", 48,1.78)
);
echo $names[0][0].": Weight: ".$names[0]
[1].", Height: ".$names[0][2].".<br>";
echo $names[1][0].": Weight: ".$names[1]
[1].", Height: ".$names[1][2].".<br>";
echo $names[2][0].": Weight: ".$names[2]
[1].", Height: ".$names[2][2].".<br>";
echo $names[3][0].": Weight: ".$names[3]
[1].", Height: ".$names[3][2].".<br>";
?>
```

Filippo: Weight: 70, Height: 1.8.
Andrea: Weight: 65, Height: 1.7.
Silvia: Weight: 45, Height: 1.75.
Marta: Weight: 48, Height: 1.78.

Or we can put a **for loop** inside *another* **for loop** to get the elements of the *$names* array:

```php
<?php
$names = array (
  array ("Filippo", 70,1.80),
  array ("Andrea", 65,1.70),
  array ("Silvia", 45,1.75),
  array ("Marta", 48,1.78)
);

for ($row = 0; $row < 4; $row++) {
  echo "<p><b>Row number $row</b></p>";
  echo "<ul>";
  for ($col = 0; $col < 3; $col++) {
    echo "<li>".$names[$row][$col]."</li>";
  }
  echo "</ul>";
}
?>
```

Row number 0

- Filippo
- 70
- 1.8

Row number 1

- Andrea
- 65
- 1.7

Row number 2

- Silvia
- 45
- 1.75

The elements of an array can be sorted alphabetically or numerically, descending or ascending.

The main sorting functions in PHP are as follows:

sort() - sorts arrays in ascending order

rsort() - sorts arrays in descending order

asort() - Sorts associative arrays in ascending order, based on value

ksort() - sorts associative arrays in ascending order, based on key

arsort() - Sorts associative arrays in descending order, based on value

krsort() - sorts associative arrays in descending order, based on key

<?php Building Real World PHP Applications ?>

PHP GLOBAL VARIABLES - SUPERGLOBALS

Some predefined variables in PHP are "*superglobal*", which means they are always accessible, regardless of *scope* - and we can access them from any function, class or file without having to set any special parameters.

The *superglobal* PHP variables are:

$GLOBALS
$_SERVER
$_REQUEST
$_POST
$_GET
$_FILES
$_ENV
$_COOKIE
$_SESSION

Let's see some of the most used ones.

$_SERVER ['PHP_SELF'] Returns the filename of the currently executing script

$_SERVER ['SERVER_ADDR'] Returns the IP address of the host server

$_SERVER ['SERVER_NAME'] Returns the host server name (such as www.aredit.com)

$_SERVER ['SERVER_SOFTWARE'] Returns the server identification string (like Apache / 2.2.24)

$_SERVER ['SERVER_PROTOCOL'] Returns the name and revision of the information protocol (like HTTP / 1.1)

<!=== Andrea Mauro Raimondi ===>

$_SERVER ['REQUEST_METHOD'] Returns the request method used to access the page (as POST)

$_SERVER ['QUERY_STRING'] Returns the query string if the page is accessed via a query string

$_SERVER ['HTTP_ACCEPT'] Returns the Accept header from the current request

$_SERVER ['HTTP_ACCEPT_CHARSET'] Returns Accept_Charset header from current request (like utf-8, ISO-8859-1)

$_SERVER ['HTTP_HOST'] Returns the Host header from the current request

$_SERVER ['HTTP_REFERER'] Returns the complete URL of the current page (not reliable because not all user-agents support it)

$_SERVER ['REMOTE_ADDR'] Returns the IP address from which the user is viewing the current page

$_SERVER ['REMOTE_HOST'] Returns the name of the host from which the user is viewing the current page

$_SERVER ['REMOTE_PORT'] Returns the port used on the user's machine to communicate with the web server

$_SERVER ['SCRIPT_FILENAME'] Returns the absolute path of the script currently running

$_SERVER ["SCRIPT_NAME"] Returns the path of the current script

$_SERVER ['SCRIPT_URI'] Returns the URI of the current page

$_REQUEST is a superglobal variable that is used to collect data after submitting an HTML form, as we have seen in PHP pages of web application used in this book.

```php
<form method="post" action="<?php echo
$_SERVER['PHP_SELF'];?>">
  Name: <input type="text" name="fname">
  <input type="submit">
</form>

<?php
if ($_SERVER["REQUEST_METHOD"] == "POST") {
    // collect value of input field
    $name = htmlspecialchars($_REQUEST['fname']);
    if (empty($name)) {
        echo "Name is empty";
    } else {
        echo $name;
    }
}
?>
```

With $_POST and $_GET you collect the information sent respectively through the POST or GET (query string) method.

<!=== Andrea Mauro Raimondi ===>

OTHER PHP FUNCTIONS

With PHP we have many functions available to manage dates, files, cookies, sessions and other aspects of server side programming. Consult the official documentation to get an idea of the extension of these features.

In this section I present some of them, among the most used and useful in my opinion:

DATE
date("Y-m-d h:i:sa", $d) allows you to format a date according to our needs.

Y represents the year in four digits

m represents the month in two digits

d represents the day in two digits

h represents the time in 12-hour format (use H for 24 hours)

i represents the minutes

a represents AM or PM

```
<!DOCTYPE html>
<html>
<body>

<?php
echo "1) Today is ".date("Y/m/d")."<br>";
echo "2) Today is ".date("Y.m.d")."<br>";
echo "3) Today is ".date("Y-m-d")."<br>";
echo "4) Today is ".date("l");
?>

</body>
</html>
```

1) Today is 2021/02/26
2) Today is 2021.02.26
3) Today is 2021-02-26
4) Today is Friday

PHP FILE HANDLING

fopen() opens a file, for reading or writing

fread() reads the contents of the file

fclose() closes the open file with fopen ()

fgets() reads one line at a time, useful when reading csv files

fwrite() writes to a file opened by fopen for writing

file_exists() checks if a file exists

```
1   <!DOCTYPE html>
2   <html>
3   <body>
4
5   <?php
6   $myfile = fopen("listofcars.txt", "r") or die("Unable to open file!");
7   // Output one line until end-of-file
8   while(!feof($myfile)) {
9     echo fgets($myfile) . "<br>";
10  }
11  fclose($myfile);
12  ?>
13
14  </body>
15  </html>
```

Displays the contents of the "listofcars.txt" file, line by line:

Mercedes-Benz – $65.04 Billion.

Toyota – $58.07 Billion.

Volkswagen – $44.89 Billion.

BMW – $40,48 Billion.

Porsche – $33.91 Billion.

Honda – $33.10 Billion.

Ford – $18.51 Billion.

Nissan – $17.92 Billion.

<!=== Andrea Mauro Raimondi ===>

SQL
MAIN COMMANDS

The **SELECT** command searchs through the records of one or more tables.

An example of a search on some fields of a table:
SELECT *field1, field2* **AS** *field alias, field3 * 12* **AS** *total*
FROM *Table*
WHERE *NomeCampo = 'textResearch'*

If you want to display all the fields of a table, use the command ***** (asterisk):
SELECT * FROM *TableName* **WHERE** *field = 'xyz'*

The **AS** command creates an *alias* of the column, the alias name is displayed, i.e., what is written after the AS command.

The **DISTINCT** command placed between SELECT and column name removes all double rows of the column:
SELECT DISTICT *fieldname* **FROM** *tableName* **WHERE** *fieldName = '2021'*

The **FROM** instruction indicates the table or tables on which operate the SELECT instruction.

<?php Building Real World PHP Applications ?>

The **WHERE** command defines the condition under which the columns are filtered
WHERE name = 'Filip'

GROUP BY
Groups the rows with the same value indicated in the clause.
SELECT *Department,* **SUM** (*Salary*)
FROM *Employees*
GROUP BY *Department*;

HAVING
Create conditions for groups created with GROUP BY, similar to the WHERE command:
SELECT *Department,* **SUM** (*Salary*)
FROM *Employees*
GROUP BY *Department*
HAVING SUM (*salary*)> *1000*

ORDER BY
Sort the records of the indicated column, if you want a descending sort, use the **DESC** command after the name of the column; the default order is **ASC** (ascending order):
ORDER BY *salary* **DESC,** LastName *ASC*;

<!=== Andrea Mauro Raimondi ===>

SEARCH CONDITIONS

BETWEEN
Selects records with values between two parameters
WHERE *Salary* **BETWEEN** *3000* **AND** *45000*

IN
Check the column values and select the ones that belong to the indicated list
WHERE *City* **IN** *('Paris', 'New York', 'Tokyo')*

LIKE
Check the value of a field, it can have the following controls (_) indicates a single character, while (**%**) indicates zero or more characters. Eg. LIKE 'abd%' or '% abc' or '% abc%' or '_abc'
WHERE *LastName* **LIKE** *'R%'*

IS NULL
WHERE *LastName* **IS (NOT) NULL**

<?php Building Real World PHP Applications ?>

AGGREGATE FUNCTIONS

Within the SELECT command you can do some columns aggregation.

COUNT: Counts records of selected column.
SELECT COUNT (*Name***) FROM** *Employees*;

SUM: Sum all records in selected column. In following example those with Name greater than R.
SELECT SUM (*Salary***) FROM** *employees* **WHERE** *Name>* 'R';

AVG: calculate average.
SELECT AVG (*Salary***) FROM** *Employees*, *Department*
WHERE *Name>* **'M' and** *Department* = '*code*';

MIN and **MAX** calculate minimum and maximum values.
SELECT MIN (*Salary***) FROM** *Employees*, *Department*
WHERE *Name>* **'M' and** *Department* = '*code*';

<!=== Andrea Mauro Raimondi ===>

JOIN

A **JOIN** clause is used to combine rows from two or more tables, based on a column related to each other.

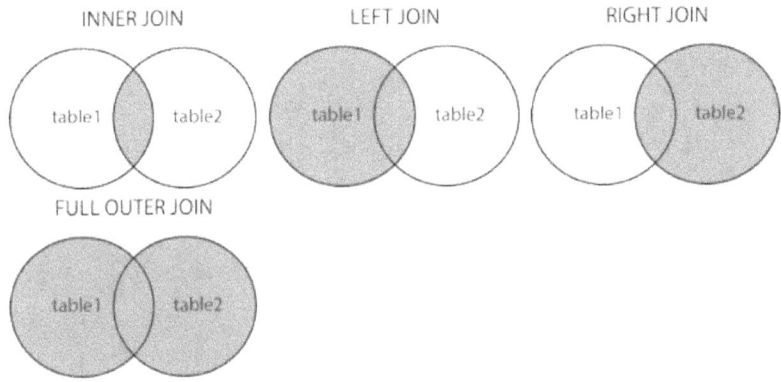

Here are the different **types of JOIN** in SQL:

(INNER) JOIN: Returns records that have matching values in *both tables*

SELECT column_name (s) FROM table1

INNER JOIN table2

ON table1.column_name = table2.column_name;

Example referred to our database

*SELECT * FROM PHP_course_products*

INNER JOIN PHP_course_categories ON PHP_course_products.idcategory = PHP_course_categories.idcategory;

All products and data relating to their category are displayed.

LEFT (OUTER) JOIN: Returns all records from the left table and matching records from the right table
SELECT column_name (s) FROM table1
LEFT JOIN table2
ON table1.column_name = table2.column_name;
Example:
SELECT * FROM PHP_course_products
LEFT JOIN PHP_course_categories ON PHP_course_products.idcategory = PHP_course_categories.idcategory;
Returns all rows in the product table and only those in the categories table that have a reference in the products table

RIGHT (OUTER) JOIN: Returns all records from the right table and matching records from the left table
SELECT column_name(s) FROM table1
RIGHT JOIN table2
ON table1.column_name = table2.column_name;
SELECT * FROM PHP_course_products
RIGHT JOIN PHP_course_categories ON PHP_course_products.idcategory = PHP_course_categories.idcategory;
Returns all rows from the categories table and only those rows from the product table that have a match through the idcategory field

FULL (OUTER) JOIN: Returns all records when there is a match in the left or right table
It is not supported by MySQL.

<!=== Andrea Mauro Raimondi ===>

INSTALL THE WEB SERVER

Fortunately, today installation of a web server is very simplified. You can use XAMPP which in one go allows you to install the Apache web server, the MySQL database in its opensource version called *MariaDB* and PHP. There are versions for Windows, Linux, and OS X.

You can find it for free download at this address:

https://www.apachefriends.org/

You will find installation videos and simple manuals:

for Linux

https://www.apachefriends.org/faq_linux.html

for Windows

https://www.apachefriends.org/faq_windows.html

for OS X

https://www.apachefriends.org/faq_osx.html

<?php Building Real World PHP Applications ?>

<!=== Andrea Mauro Raimondi ===>

REFERENCE

PHP
https://www.php.net/

MySQL
https://www.mysql.com/

PHPMyAdmin
https://www.phpmyadmin.net/

Apache Mysql (MariaDB) PHP
https://www.apachefriends.org

Template area back office
AdminLTE3: https://adminlte.io/themes/v3/

Template website
https://templatemo.com/

Write me info@aredit.com and I send all PHP code used in this book.

OTHER RESOURCES

List of color names and hexadecimal code
https://www.w3schools.com/colors/colors_hex.asp

PHP usage examples
https://www.w3schools.com/php/

Working with Images
GIMP
https://www.gimp.org

<!=== Andrea Mauro Raimondi ===>

For consulting, courses, customized web application, write to info@aredit.com or visit https://www.aredit.com

I create for the web since 1999.

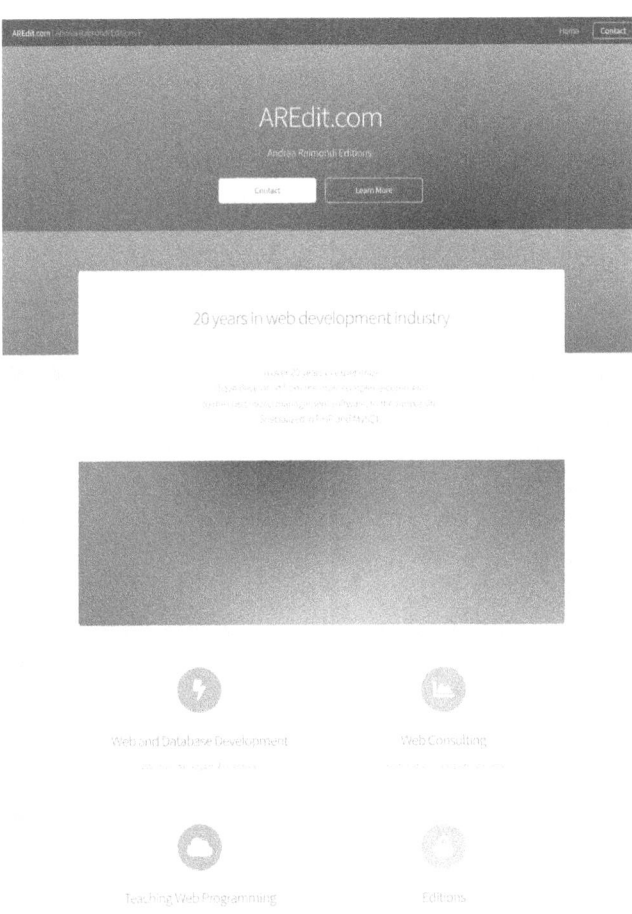

<?php Building Real World PHP Applications ?>

© 2021 Andrea Mauro Raimondi
https://www.aredit.com
info@aredit.com